Life Cycle Assessment – Recent Advances and New Perspectives

Edited by Tamás Bányai and Péter Veres

Published in London, United Kingdom

Life Cycle Assessment - Recent Advances and New Perspectives
http://dx.doi.org/10.5772/intechopen.107596
Edited by Tamás Bányai and Péter Veres

Contributors
Sergio Rafael Bravo Orellana, Ali Bahadori-Jahromi, Augustine Blay-Armah, Anastasia Mylona, Golnaz Mohebbi, Miguel Chen Austin, Kimberly Beermann, Carol Monticelli, Katja Malovrh Rebec, Janez Turk, Cevza Candan, Sedef Uncu Akı, Banu Nergis, Neslihan Sebla Önder

First published in London, United Kingdom, 2023 by IntechOpen
IntechOpen is the global imprint of INTECHOPEN LIMITED, registered in England and Wales, registration number: 11086078, 5 Princes Gate Court, London, SW7 2QJ, United Kingdom

British Library Cataloguing-in-Publication Data
A catalogue record for this book is available from the British Library

Additional hard and PDF copies can be obtained from orders@intechopen.com

Life Cycle Assessment - Recent Advances and New Perspectives
Edited by Tamás Bányai and Péter Veres
p. cm.
Print ISBN 978-1-80356-878-2
Online ISBN 978-1-80356-879-9
eBook (PDF) ISBN 978-1-80356-880-5

Meet the editors

Tamás Bányai received a master's degree in 1993 and a Ph.D. in 1999, both from the University of Miskolc, Hungary, where he is currently a full-time professor. He has 30 years of teaching and research experience in the design and control of materials handling systems and supply chain management, with special emphasis on heuristic optimization of large-scale systems. He has published more than 200 research papers, book chapters, and conference proceedings. He has been a member and manager of more than fifty national and international R&D projects. Away from academia, Prof. Bányai's other interests include playing the piano and taking photographs.

Péter Veres received a master's degree as a Logistics Engineer and a Mining- and Geotechnical Engineer in 2014 and a Ph.D. in Informatics from the University of Miskolc, Hungary, in 2014 and 2020, respectively. He is currently a senior lecturer at the same university. He has more than 10 years of teaching and research experience in the optimization of logistic systems in warehousing and layout design using heuristic optimization and simulation. He has published fifty research papers, book chapters and conference proceedings. He has participated in more than ten mainly industrial R&D works supplemented by a few international R&D projects. Currently, one of his primary research interests is the integration of artificial intelligence (AI) systems into logistics. Outside of academic life, Dr. Veres likes to play and create board games and goes mineral collecting in the mountains.

Contents

Preface

This book offers a selection of chapters on life cycle assessment, promoting new research results in the field. Authors from the United Kingdom, Panama, Italy, Slovenia, Turkey, and Peru have contributed work examples and case studies from their research in life cycle assessment.

The book covers six topics, determined by the theoretical and practical aspects of life cycle assessment.

Chapter 1, "Life Cycle Assessment in Architecture as Decisional Tool in the Design Stage", focuses on the entire life cycle of buildings in the context of materials, components, energy, and resource consumption.

Chapter 2, "Life Cycle Assessment of Buildings: An End-of-Life Perspective", discusses the problems of building demolition waste and proposes potential appropriate waste strategies to minimize generated waste. The authors developed an assessment framework, which they tested using a case study of a supermarket building. The study shows the impact of processing and transportation of demolished waste materials on carbon emissions and validated that steel waste recycling has the best environmental benefits. The detailed assessment approach in this chapter can be adopted for different real-world projects.

Chapter 3, "Including Nature-Based Success Measurement Criteria in the Life Cycle Assessment", shows how biomimicry principles can improve current life cycle impact assessment tools. The authors conclude that most assessment tools continue to be developed under the "reducing unsustainability" paradigm, where different approaches present great potential for an "achieving sustainability" paradigm. Their research results are validated by two case studies focusing on built environments: net-zero-buildings and sustainable construction projects.

Chapter 4, "Life Cycle Assessment as a Next Level of Transparency in Denim Manufacturing", demonstrates how life cycle assessment can be used to make processes more transparent. The authors present the methodology of building a suitable life cycle assessment model and use the data to compare different products and production practices in the denim industry. The proposed methodological framework makes it possible to calculate the impacts of product developers' and/or designers' choices in denim manufacturing.

Chapter 5, "Pathway toward Sustainable Winter Road Maintenance (Case Study)", discusses the environmental impacts of winter road maintenance using life cycle assessment methodology. The case study shows that an innovative road-weather information system makes it possible to optimize maintenance operations, which can lead to the use of less salt, thus significantly decreasing the environmental impact of winter road maintenance. The proposed approach takes the required processes of winter road maintenance, the mobility of vehicles passing the road, and their fuel consumption into consideration. The results of the comparative life cycle assessment analysis show that the proposed road-weather information system can lead to a 25% reduction in environmental footprints.

Chapter 6, "The Life Cycle in Startup Valuation", analyzes the life cycle of startups. The author categorizes the startups by type of innovation, focusing on process innovation and disruptive innovation. The lifecycles of the startups are compared in terms of risk, duration, and investment level.

The aim of this book is to help students as well as managers and researchers to understand and appreciate the concept, design, and implementation of life cycle assessment solutions.

The editors thank the chapter authors for their scientific contributions. The chapters were edited and published following a rigorous selection process. We also wish to thank and acknowledge the many individuals who helped us throughout the editorial process that made this book possible.

Tamás Bányai and Péter Veres
Institute of Logistics,
University of Miskolc,
Miskolc, Hungary

Chapter 1

Life Cycle Assessment in Architecture as Decisional Tool in the Design Stage

Carol Monticelli

Abstract

The horizon of sustainability calls into question extremely complex phenomena, both in terms of social, economic, and cultural transformations, and in terms of the ecological implications of building activity in its wide territorial and temporal extension, and in terms of and the techniques to refer to. On this last aspect, in particular, today it is necessary to counteract the tendency toward an inconsiderate simplification of the aforementioned complex phenomena, because this simplistic approach is precisely the cause of the often trivialized and sometimes radically wrong interpretations. The chapter develops the theme of environmental sustainability precisely in this complex perspective, assuming the consideration of the entire life cycle of building products, whether they are materials, components, or buildings, as an inescapable reference horizon and the measurement of energy and resource consumption and of the impacts that are determined along the life cycle (Life Cycle Assessment—LCA) as the main tool for assessing the concrete sustainability of design choices with rigor and scientific basis.

Keywords: life cycle assessment, built environment, architecture, buildings, life cycle thinking, design process, regenerative development

1. Introduction

The shift of attention in the design choices derives from the interpretative evolution of the environmental problem and from the new intervention approach: from an *ex post* impact assessment, with the aim of limiting the damage and environmental risks of already existing works and processes, to an *ex ante*, through prevention and research of concepts and strategies aimed at analyzing a building and its parts upstream of the construction process, with the aim of designing an eco-efficient or low environmental impact system. This is a different approach from the practice that has characterized the building industry in recent decades, particularly attentive to a complex and at the same time delicate "environmental system," often exploited to the limit and erroneously considered unalterable: the changes undergone by the ecosystem are known, as a result of human actions, and the visible repercussions caused by these transformations, such as global warming, climate change, soil acidification, water eutrophication, and depletion of the ozone layer. Architecture does not remain extraneous to this framework of problems: it is a manifestation of human activities. Therefore, designing and building according to the criteria of sustainability essentially means dealing with the principles that make the balance between use of resources and environmental impact feasible.

Ecologically responsible design has been acquired in many scientific-disciplinary sectors of architecture and is currently the subject of studies and research by the scientific sector of architectural technology and the building production sector. In these areas, two distinct aspects of the problem are considered in particular: on the one hand, the definition of environmental design strategies for buildings and settlements, and on the other hand, the environmental impacts of building products and of buildings as a whole in order to guide the strategies design them. There is therefore a change of hierarchy between the paradigms of the project, which must be rethought and calibrated on new bases and scenarios of a vision over time of the life of the built artifact. The theme is not only the design of the building, but also of the life of a building, in which the temporal and spatial dimensions are fundamental and must be declined on the different scales of the built environment. The role of duration and maintenance scheduling in buildings is decisive on the life cycle from the early stages of the project; they are aspects closely linked to the technologies used, which in turn are consequences of the environmental context: which technology for which duration? Which technology for which context?

To support the ongoing renewal of the design process, Life Cycle Thinking (LCT) is a criterion through which it is possible to carry out actions or make decisions with awareness of the entire life cycle of the building, the process, and the product in question. It can be defined as a current of thought that compares a product or a process to a living organism, which is born, grows, dies [1]. Through this similarity, the life of a building and its process can be considered as a sequence of phases: that of design, that of extraction and processing of raw materials, that of packaging and distribution to final uses, that of construction and system of individual components, that of use and management and, last but not least, the end-of-life phase, which can be transformed into the first phase of new forms of life, through reuse and recycling. The life cycle of an organism or a process interacts with the surrounding environment, and the interaction with adjacent systems can be assimilated to a chain of flows with inputs (substances for processing, energy, human work, technology, money, etc.) and output (waste substances from processing, energy from network losses, waste materials, etc.), in close contact and exchange with the environmental, social, and economic spheres.

For the construction sector, this approach takes root and is accepted with the delay in the implementation of innovation typical of the sector. The need to evaluate the characteristics of building materials first emerges, then the LCT is implemented by the production chain, and slowly and, often, with actions that are not yet well defined methodologically, the approach to analyzing the life cycle of systems is recognized constructive and buildings as the only viable way to understand the wealth of problems that pervade the design of the eco-efficient building. We can state that many companies, in particular those aware of their harmful load on the environment, are moving (since the seventies), also under the obligation of international agreements on the reduction of environmental impacts, to pursue objectives of a more controlled production; others are moving toward the proposal of more or less "green" products and components, whose effective eco-efficiency must in any case be verified beyond the production phase, once inserted in a building context. But this is not enough, clear guidelines toward higher environmental goals and techniques for the prevention of environmental pollution are still faltering, many attitudes are only palliatives, with an unconscious still destructive and short-term perspective. Efforts in developing eco-efficiency assessment methods for buildings are appreciable, but still too fragmented and ineffective.

The analysis of the life cycle of an entire building presupposes the decomposition into underestimations of the components that constitute it. This operation may appear simple, but it must be recognized that on an operational level it becomes a very complex practice, due to the innumerable amount of information that the many actors involved in the project must provide simultaneously. A possible approach consists in assimilating building components as industrial products, since they are made in manufacturing industries and, only later, delivered to the construction site and assembled as pieces of an industrial product [2]. This affirmation presupposes a way of building with dry assembly technologies, therefore of combining industrial products, but it could also be traced back to traditional shipyards. A building, built with traditional or advanced technologies, is in any case a complex system, whose variables are not always predictable and controllable like an industrial product; it is a system that must also include esthetic, functional, and social aspects. The environmental assessment of a building must not be reduced to the sum of the environmental impacts of the individual components, since a building is not a car which, once built, can be delivered anywhere in the world and works; the building is built in a precise context and the technical and construction choices determine its duration (prolonged over time compared to other everyday objects we have), which also varies according to the user and the weather conditions with which it lives.

Among the many methods of analyzing environmental quality at different scales of the built environment, the Life Cycle Assessment (LCA) environmental assessment methodology is the reference for the detailed and objective quantification of the environmental impacts of a product and of the building along the entire cycle of life, through the quantification of incoming material and energy flows and outgoing polluting emissions in the phases of extraction of raw materials, transport, production, installation, use and management, decommissioning and end of life. The LCA methodology takes into consideration all types of impact in a complete framework of indicators and all phases of the life cycle, up to closing the cycle in the case of recycling at the end of its life, with the balance of the advantages of avoiding further consumption of materials and energy. The LCA assessment, structured in phases, in addition to the definition of the objectives of its application and of the object to be analyzed, provides for an accurate inventory of all the processes of the life cycle of the analyzed product, which translates into a flow diagram with the quantification of matter, water, incoming energy and outgoing emissions of substances into the air, water, and soil. The latter are translated, through a characterization, into environmental impacts (greenhouse effect, thinning of the ozone layer, etc.) and subsequently evaluated, with a score that indicates the severity of the damage, in order to contextualize the environmental damage to a specific reality territorial.

It is therefore necessary that, in addition to understanding the environmental problem, metabolizing the principles of design aimed at the life cycle, strategies and methods are structured aimed at optimizing the sustainable project first and then the eco-efficient architectural product.

2. New approaches for environmentally responsible architectural design

In order to easily understand how it can be designed to protect the environment, a building must be thought of as an ecosystem through which natural resources and semifinished products, components and systems coexist in a continuous cycle of flows (of matter and energy), within which a series of subsystems regulate the flow of one or more types of resources. It is important to understand that the presence of a building in the environment has a large impact both upstream of the construction, before the operational phase, and downstream, at the end of its life span. Focusing on a building and its potential impacts on the environment, it is necessary to consider the two streams of resource flows: those *upstream*, as inputs for the building ecosystem, and those *downstream*, as those that flow out as output from the ecosystem from it. The flow of resources begins upstream (input) with the entire construction and manufacturing industry sector, with the production of building materials, and continues throughout the life span of the building, in which the objective is to create an environment sustainable and healthy for human well-being and related activities. At the end of its useful life, the building must be considered, right from the design and the choices of construction technologies, as a "mine" of components (output flow), to be modified or transformed, for other new buildings or uses. The law of conservation of the mass of Antoine Lavoisier [3] also applies to the building ecosystem, according to which, over a long period, the resources that have entered will eventually come out, presumably transformed. This transformation from entrance to exit is caused by many mechanical processes or human interventions during the use phase of buildings.

It is therefore essential to know and quantify the flows in order to pursue an economy of resources, materials and energy, through the reduction, reuse, and recycling of input flows for a building. Paying attention to the economy of resources, the designer must know how to choose materials and components, knowing the energy content (nonrenewable or renewable) and the environmental impacts as well as evaluating the application context. It must contemplate the containment of nonrenewable resources in the construction and management of buildings, in which a continuous flow of resources, natural and man-made, is generated in and out of the building itself. The concept of Triple Zero, for example, promotes a "concentrate" of sustainability to be considered in the design of a building or a product: production and materials at 0 km, 0 CO_2 emissions, reduction to 0 of waste products, and closure of cycles.

The three strategies contemplated by the principle of resource economy are energy saving, water saving, and material conservation; each focuses on a particular resource needed for building construction and management (**Figures 1–3**).

In order to optimize the flows in the various phases of the building process in the design phase, Life Cycle Design (LCD) suggests a methodology for analyzing the construction process and its environmental impact, phase by phase. The same sequence is necessary to operate the inventory of the substances involved (input and output) in the production processes involved in each phase of the life cycle, the initial investigation level of the Life Cycle Assessment methodology, a fundamental part of the LCD thanks to which it is possible to extrapolate the data and information on which to base the environmental impact assessment methods, to be used in the architectural design phase.

The preconstruction phase includes the choice of the site, the design phase, the production processes of materials, and components for the building system up to the delivery on site, excluding the installation. According to the strategy of sustainable design, the environmental consequences generated by the architectural project, the orientation, and the impact on the landscape and that of the materials used are examined. The procurement of building materials also generates an impact on the environment: the harvesting of trees could generate deforestation; the extraction of mineral

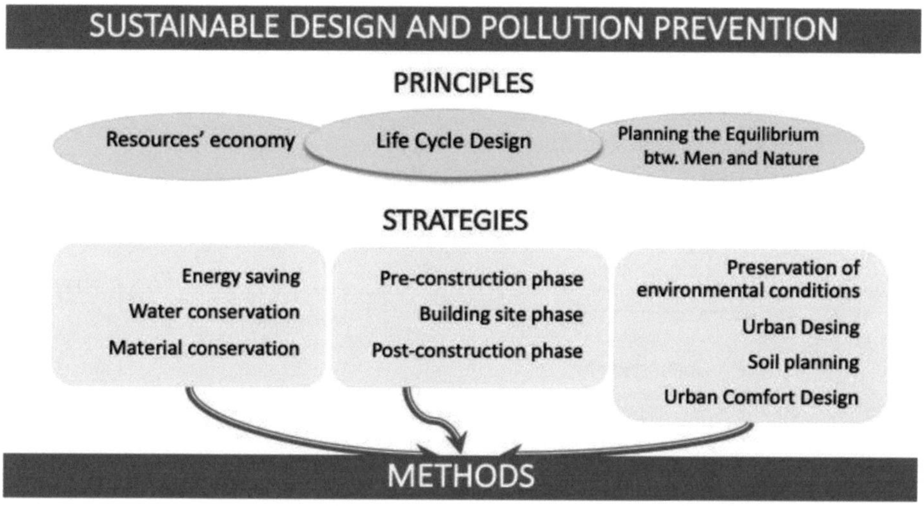

Figure 1.
Conceptual scheme for a life cycle design (LCD) and for the prevention of environmental pollution in architecture.

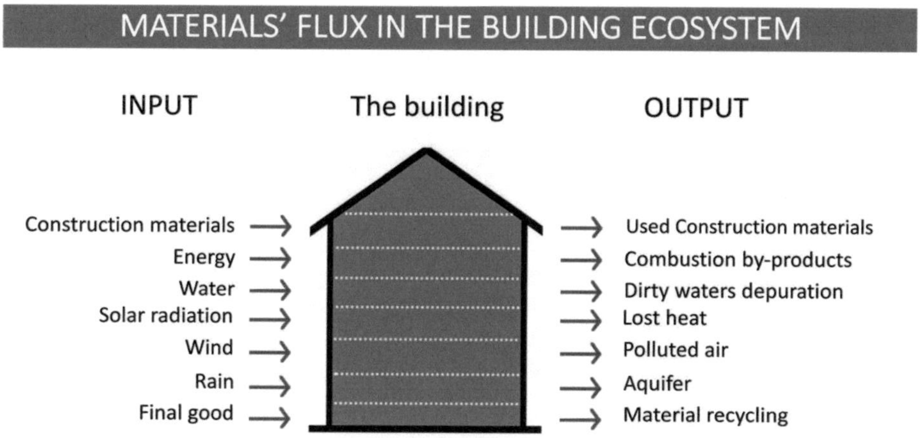

Figure 2.
The flows of substances in input and output in the "ecosystem" of the building.

resources (iron for steel, bauxite for aluminum, sand, gravel, and limestone for cement) cause, in addition to a great visual impact, the erosion of entire mountains or chasms and disturb stability soils, as well as generating acoustic and atmospheric pollution (e.g. fine dust); even the transport of these materials can be a highly polluting activity, depending on the weight and distance from the site. The manufacturing phase of construction products requires large quantities of energy, so much so that in many situations it is highly energy consuming and polluting compared to the energy required by buildings for their air conditioning during use: for example, the steel production chains and aluminum require a high level of energy, for smelting at high temperatures.

The construction phase and the operational phase refer to the phase of the life cycle, in which the building has been physically built and is in use and management.

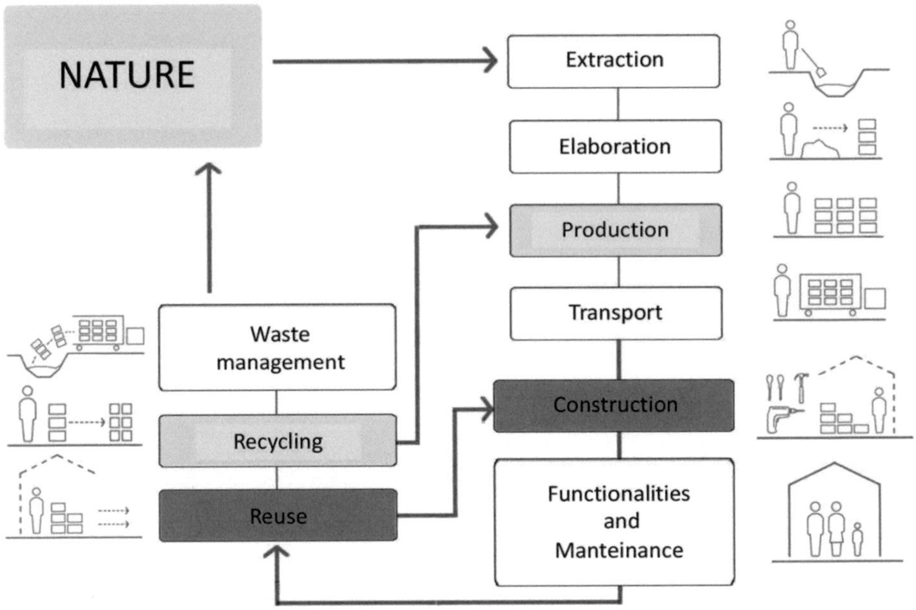

Figure 3.
A sustainable building life cycle.

In the eco-efficient design strategy, the operating methods of the construction and management processes must be investigated in the design phase in order to identify technical, plant, and operational solutions aimed at reducing the consumption of resources. In the investigation of this phase, the possible long-term effects of the built environment on the health of its users are also considered. Works that could significantly contribute to the reduction of the energy demand in this phase are the rehabilitation of the existing envelopes, a more adequate design of the envelopes in new buildings, a regulation of the summer air conditioning, the introduction of automated management systems and a use, where possible of renewable energies. The restoration of the envelopes allows the reduction of consumption for heating and is a binding condition for the installation of summer air conditioning. The post-consumer, or end-of-life, phase begins when a building's useful life has ended. In this phase, the building materials, demolished or preferably disassembled, are transformed into resources for other buildings or waste to be returned to nature. The eco-efficient design strategy focuses on reducing construction waste (which currently includes 60% of solid waste in landfills), reusing systems and components, and recycling building materials.

In addition to the requirements for a sustainable project and the characteristics of a sustainable material, the performance of a technological system, of a sustainable construction site, established starting from 1999 according to Agenda 21—CIB on Sustainable Construction, must be evaluated, which consist of:

- Choice and use of local materials, i.e. a sustainable material, component, or technological system in a specific physical location is not always sustainable in another; the reference to local cultures and ways of use as opposed to the approval of ways of building, as an international style, must be taken into consideration;

- Marking of the components, i.e. a widespread criterion in industrial production which allows tracing the manufacturer of the component, its technical characteristics and the interface and operating methods, to which will also be added the characteristics of environmental impact;

- Recyclable materials: recycling, together with reuse and reuse strategies, constitutes an obligatory step toward the sustainability of the production cycles of building materials;

- Minimization of transport, evaluating the impact of the construction activity on the transport system and on the quality of life of the entire context in which it operates;

- Construction systems that can be easily assembled/disassembled, which considers a modular or component-based design approach, contemplating the construction site as a place for assembly and disassembly of components of industrial origin rather than as a place for processing raw materials (water, sand, gravel, and cement) or of materials (bricks, blocks, interposed, etc.) that make up structures, closures, and partitions;

- Reusable construction systems, which imply a technologically complex challenge, which requires an update of the principles of assembly and prefabrication, but above all of correct selective disassembly of the components to be reused;

- Maintainability over time: the estimate of the useful life of the building product, unlike the industrial product, is measured in many decades or centuries, so it is important to have an in-depth knowledge of the aspects of durability and to counteract the degradation of materials, predict the life of the components, and manage the inevitable failures, pursuing the lengthening of the useful life [4] (**Figure 4**).

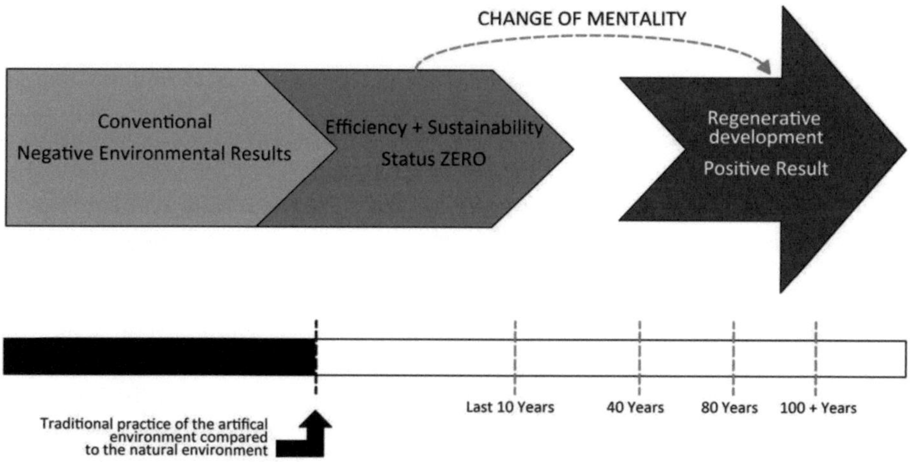

Figure 4.
Shifting the approach from traditional business to positive environmental outcomes.

3. The characterization of systems for the building design: the geographical and matter context

Considering the breadth of material possibilities and technical solutions offered by the market for the design and construction of the building, it is a difficult task to identify choices with characteristics suitable for the reference context, from a functional, economic, and above all environmental point of view. It is necessary for designers to have a conscious and coherent knowledge of the characteristics of building components, their expected performance and their environmental impact, and a critical observation of their real validity, for the purpose of making informed technological choices. The market seems to reward products that do not address the complexity of the problem, but only buffer it apparently, often responding to trends or "symptoms of the moment." This attitude only creates further confusion superficiality and lack of clarity. The choice of a component must not only be determined by its compliance with a function, but in the broader perspective of the use that will be made of it, a specific use linked to the environmental, temporal, and social context. In addition to the question "which form for which function," "which technology for which building," and "which material for which context" must immediately be correlated. The context, as well as in a static sense (the physical place), is linked to the use and users in a dynamic sense, with modifications and different approaches over time. A building arises from a specific, localized project pertinent to a technical and material culture, which is, even if not deriving from the whole, at least in part related to the society that produces it.

It is not enough to characterize the choice of materials and components for the building on the basis of product certifications, the CE quality marking of the manufacturing company or on technical sheets validated by scores on the level of eco-compatibility of the product. Extreme awareness of the environmental profile of the component contextualized with respect to the building in which it will be located is required; a choice of a component must be verified every time it is decided to insert it in a building in relation to the specific geographical, urban/suburban context. Each project, therefore each building, has its own story with respect to others or with respect to the context.

4. Environmental impacts in the life cycle of buildings

The construction of a building causes effects on the environment not only in the construction phase but also throughout the building process: the impacts generated by production, from the use phase, up to the impacts determined by the decommissioning of the building and the end of life of materials.

Among the main types of impact we mention air pollution, mainly due to the combustion processes used for the production of energy; chemical and biological pollution of water, mostly caused by urban, industrial, agricultural, and livestock waste; noise pollution, particularly important in urban centers and near airports and communication routes; the effects on the landscape and on the territorial structure due to the construction of large industrial and energy plants, the construction of infrastructures such as ports, airports, railways, and motorways; and the health and environmental effects, due to accidents that can occur in plants with a significant risk, such as nuclear power plants, hydroelectric plants, and chemical plants. These environmental effects have a common feature: they can be quantified. This makes it possible to use scientific methods to be able to assess their extent.

There are numerous types of impact, the global effects (greenhouse effect and acid rain) and the effects on the balance of ecosystems, which are only partially quantifiable and which therefore must be analyzed with empirical, conservative, semiquantitative or, depending on the case, simply dictated approaches by public acceptability requirements.

The pure scientific method is not sufficient to give a complete answer to the numerous environmental problems generated by the design of manufactured articles; however, attempts are underway to optimize the assessment of environmental impacts, the main objective of which is to investigate the compatibility between a given project and the environment. Some precautions must be taken at several levels in the building sector, to foresee (and not only ascertain) all the possible causes of environmental impact: at the design level by analyzing different alternatives of materials and technical elements, to obtain the suitable solution, with the best performance and minimum consumption; at the manufacturing industry level to control the quality of the production process and reduce waste and emissions into the environment during the processing chain; in the construction phase of a building, with an improvement in times and construction site processes; in the operational and management phase of the product, with an optimization of consumption (thermal, electrical) for air conditioning, lighting, and household appliances.

4.1 Impacts in the production phase

Building materials and components are the result of the transformation of raw materials, using energy. From the raw material to the semifinished products, to the finished product, to reach the waste product at the end of its function, each intermediate phase necessary for the processing of the material requires energy which accumulates in the product (as a quantity of incorporated energy) or is released in the environment in the form of heat. In going through the various subphases of the production processes of a building material, one learns how all the levels contribute to the impacts on the environment. In the procurement of raw materials, enormous quantities of materials from quarries and mines are eroded, disfiguring the landscape, as well as consuming nonrenewable materials. Furthermore, it is unthinkable to foresee the future use of only renewable sources, since these too, in addition to not being inexhaustible, have effects on the territory: to build in wood, extensive cultivation of trees is needed to procure raw materials. Once again, the importance of placing the choices in the context of the project and evaluating the exploitation of raw materials, whether exhaustible or inexhaustible, is evident.

The *impacts relating to transport* should not be underestimated. Unfortunately, today, with the globalization of markets and the evolution of construction technology, it is no longer possible to think about the local procurement of materials. Above all, given the heterogeneity of the products on the market, it is no longer easy to check the origin of the same, so the movements that a product carries out in the early stages of its life, up to its transfer to the construction site for which it is intended, cause significant impacts on the environment.

The *actual manufacturing phase* generates, due to the consumption of energy and emissions of waste materials and harmful substances, the greatest pollution in the supply chain, as well as in the entire life cycle of a building. The willingness of companies to reduce the resources and energy used (mostly lost during processes in the form of heat) is slowly entering, thanks also to actions coordinated by trade associations, as well as by national regulations; however, a certain difficulty remains in the management of waste from manufacturing scraps or industrial processes.

4.2 Impacts during the operational phase

There is a clear urgency to intervene on management consumption (heating, air conditioning, lighting, ventilation, consumption of household appliances, etc.) with greater attention to the efficiency of production processes and impacts on the environment.

Carbon dioxide emissions, responsible for climate change, are proportional to primary energy consumption, with different weights depending on the primary energy carrier (methane, LPG, petrol, diesel, fuel oil, and coal). It is necessary to analyze the consumption of primary energy, for the assessment of the environmental impacts of the national energy system. The forms of pollution linked to local energy consumption, due to the emission of toxic substances such as unburnt products such as carbon monoxide (CO), such as nitrogen oxides (NOx), and such as dust and specifically the articulated (PM10) are dangerous to human health, locally and in the short term, have practically no effect on the global climate.

However, pollutants are generated in concentrated points, such as industrial centers and urban areas. Around every large city, there is a cloud containing polluted gases and dust, noise and light disturbances, with local phenomena affecting health. The widespread distribution of pollution sources makes a systemic approach to their management difficult. We have to think that from these poles, pollution spreads over the entire planet.

Works that could contribute considerably are the rehabilitation of the existing envelopes, a more adequate design of the envelopes in new buildings; a regulation of the summer conditioning; the introduction of automated management systems and the use, where possible, of renewable energies. The restoration of the envelopes allows the reduction of consumption for heating and is a binding condition for the installation of summer air conditioning.

4.3 The post-consumption phase

At the end of the life span of single systems/components or of the whole building, we are faced with enormous volumes of waste, if we consider the high quantity of building materials used every year.

Due to the variety of substances contained in construction products, disposal operations are not always easy to plan: there are more and more substances that are highly harmful to the environment and human health, so disposal in landfills is not enough, but it is necessary to resort to the collection of special waste. And furthermore, while planning the demolition and disposal, right from the design stage, the time between the production stage and decommissioning is too long. Therefore, it is desirable to opt for preventive actions, i.e. designing buildings with reversible construction methods, which facilitate the disassembly and selective demolition of the parts, allowing, where possible, material recycling operations. It is necessary to introduce Design for Disassembling (DfD) among the design paradigms, trying to predict, in the design of a product, the scenario at the end of its useful life: this principle also affects the choice of construction technologies and materials and components, whose durability must be known. Being able to predict the treatment of a material or component at the end of its service life can imply the improvement of the manufacturing process and the orientation of construction choices toward precise technologies.

A material can be made with reduced impacts in the production chain, but, if landfill is destined, the initial advantage, in a life cycle balance, is compromised.

Predicting today an end of life in place only in a few years takes on a forecasting nature: now we know the means and processes of treatment in current practice, but the future scenario, through technological innovation and more in-depth knowledge of the temporality of new materials, can be completely different.

5. Application strategies in architecture

An essential certainty that is spreading in architecture and construction is the importance of disseminating knowledge of the long-term environmental impacts of materials, components, and technological solutions for buildings. It is now known how a design choice, in relation to materials and technological solutions and their production chain, can generate environmental impacts comparable to decades of energy consumption by a building, built without any energy-saving criteria. However, awareness-raising propaganda is still needed to make people understand how the application of the LCA methodology in architecture and the use of synthetic indicators of environmental impact must serve to optimize the life cycle of the "building system," in order to understand, from time to time and for each specific case, what are the phases on which to act to reduce environmental impacts. In the approach to the use of LCA in architecture, a complete optimization of all phases of the life cycle is not easily achievable; therefore, it is essential to define clear optimization objectives. If choices of materials and components are made by paying attention to the environmental impacts of the production and transport phase, to improve the pre-consumption phase, it is not obvious that this will lead to equally low impacts in the management and maintenance phase and at the end of life. The single strategy envisages pursuing a result with different characteristics, as well as contrasting ones, with respect to the result obtainable with a different strategy. The choice of strategy must be made in relation to the design context and the type of building, its form and function, its expected useful life. The translation of these concepts in terms of the LCA methodology consists in the definition of the objectives and boundaries of the system to be analyzed.

An important concept is that the role of the LCA environmental assessment must continue in parallel with the building design phases and not be just a final check, and it must be an operational and decision support tool with respect to the set objectives.

The types of LCA analysis that can be adopted in general are different, depending on the sectors involved or the phases considered, or the levels to be analyzed (material scale, component scale, technological subsystem scale, and building scale). The application of the LCA analysis can be done in detail in relation to the purpose and objectives of the study. The main levels of detail are:

a. **A product LCA** (defined as "simplified"), in which only the product in question is considered, not the secondary production processes, the impacts of the raw materials, fuels, and electricity used exclusively in the product line are calculated (are not considered process inputs and outputs deriving from upstream production, that of the raw material in the fundamental process); this analysis is rather simplified, and it uses generic data, both quantitative and qualitative, to make the evaluations as simple as possible. The purpose of the product LCA is to essentially provide some guidelines for the processes under investigation. Sometimes, however, the level of accuracy does not allow obtaining reliability on the results. The first objective to pursue is therefore to identify the information that can be omitted without compromising the result. The simplification of the method is based on three stages, which are iteratively linked:

- Investigation: identification of the most important parts of the life cycle or those with the largest data gaps;
- Simplification: from the results of the survey the work is set on the parts of the system considered most important;
- Evaluation of reliability: it is verified that the simplifications introduced do not significantly reduce the reliability of the overall result.

b. **An extended technology LCA** (defined as "selection") in which the products and processes correlated to the process under analysis are evaluated, used for raw materials and semifinished products during the fundamental process; however, at this level some minor processes are left out, it is commonly used when key actions for environmental improvement in the life cycle of products must be identified, in specific process parts. Its main feature is that of making use of calculation codes that help to manage the implementation of the LCA, referring to data already available from databases or estimated with approximation. From the obtainend results, and following a sensitivity analysis, the critical data on which it is necessary to intervene to improve their environmental quality are identified. It is a rapid system that allows to evaluate the important aspects of the life cycle, on which focusing attention.

c. **A complete LCA** (defined as "detailed"), which includes all the phases of the object in question and the related processes (it also implies processes of extraction and transport of fuels to the place of use, processes of production of equipment and buildings used in the various processes, direct impacts, indirect impacts, land use by the industrial warehouses where production takes place, etc.); this type of analysis involves examining many processes and, consequently, an even greater number of impacts on the environment. A detailed study foresees an improvement in data quality, instead of referring to standard data or secondary data; it is desirable to proceed with the collection and use of case-specific data provided by the companies themselves. It is the longest and most expensive method, but it is the one that provides the greatest reliability.

In the specificity of the LCA applied to the building and its parts, it would obviously be desirable to apply a complete or detailed level of study (c) of a building, quantifying: from the quantities of materials for the main structures and subsystems, going down in detail, up to understanding the quantities of materials for the electric cables, for the switches, for the sanitary fixtures, the pipes of the systems, and every single/small part of the product. The completeness of the application also implies considering all phases of the life cycle of the building, and for each component involved also its durability or duration and its possible end of life: all these aspects must be balanced in the LCI. For various reasons set out below, this level is not realistically usable in the building sector: information, of a design and construction nature, and the quantities relating to all parts of the building are not easily prosecutable.

In most of the cases and in the widespread practice, all the executive technical choices from the design phase are not always known, since they are often decided during the construction.

It is not the goal of the LCA application to architectural design and construction to exhaust the completeness of the data down to the smallest detail, rather than to use the potential of the methodology to compare similar solutions or contributions from different life cycle phases and understand where they are concentrated the major environmental impacts of the case considered.

The objective of the LCA applied to the building or its parts is not aimig to reach a single absolute final score, aimed at itself, but to allow for improvement judgments where an impact imbalance or, at least, awareness emerges (it often happens that in order to improve one aspect from the point of view of impacts, one is forced to accept the worsening of other aspects and, in this case, the comparison serves to understand which aspect causes less environmental damage).

In the construction sector, the utility of the comparative LCA between buildings, between subsystems, between different material, technological, and structural solutions for the same subsystem, between different components but with performances (mechanical, thermal, acoustic, fire resistance, etc.) clearly emerges at the same; from each comparison the limits and potential of each system considered emerge and, through an interpretative analysis of the LCA results, alternative solutions, or optimizations of some design aspects can be evaluated.

However, referring to the application studies of the sector available in the literature, the most widespread application sees the level of study with enlarged technology or selection (b).

For which they typically conduct:

- Comparative LCA of building materials, for one or more phases of the life cycle;
- Comparative LCA of technological components or systems, for one or more phases of the life cycle;
- Comparative LCA of building subsystems, for one or more phases of the life cycle;
- LCA of a building, in which the impacts of the different phases of the life cycle are compared: the pre-use phase with the phase of transporting materials from the company to the construction site, the construction phase, the management phase, with maintenance, end-of-life stage.

In the sector there are studies of application of the LCA methodology to the scale of the material and the component, which can be considered with a complete level of detail (c), with the aim of building the entire production process, from the cradle to the gate, therefore from the procurement of raw materials, to industrial processes up to packaging, considering all branches of the chain of flows with the environmental impacts of machinery (and their construction), the use of the land by industry and, upstream, by industries or sourcing quarries of raw materials, etc. These assessments serve to create the process entry relating to the environmental impact for a defined unit of building material (1 kg and 1 cubic meter of material), which constitute or are comparable to the entries contained in the reference databases for the LCA. Therefore, it can be affirmed that in the evaluations of an extended technological type, at the building scale, certainly many processes are included which, taken individually, can be considered as results of complete LCA. Regarding the LCA applications that compare phases of the life cycle of the building, scientific research works emerge that specifically analyze single phases, the pre-use phase of the building rather than the end-of-life phase of the building and components, with the objective of understanding, in one case, the production processes that have the greatest impact on the environmental impact of building construction [5–7] and, in the second case, the possible end-of-life scenarios and the advantages or limitations of each scenario (landfill, waste-to-energy, recycling, or reuse) [8–11].

The use of LCA as a methodology to support the design and optimization of production chains, in general, can be traced back to the early 1990s [12–16] and as a methodology with calculation codes that can be optimized for the building sector since 1996, at the building scale [17–25] and the scale of the material and component [26–31].

The wide use of comparative LCA in architectural design has been intensifying since 1996, with an increase in application cases, found in scientific literature, from year to year. There are now many application cases at the building scale: one trend sees the use of the methodology for assessing the environmental impact on a building, as a single-case study [32–35], which highlights the different impacts in the phases of the life cycle or the incidence of the various building systems with respect to the overall environmental and energy impact (e.g. the impact on the environmental effects of the structure or building materials respects the entire life cycle of the building [36]), as well as on several buildings compared to each other, whether they are residential buildings [37–42] or tertiary [43, 44], school [45] or public [46–48].

A widely codified use of the comparative LCA can be found at the subsystem scale, in which technologies with different materials or technological alternatives of products are compared, for example, two different structural systems are compared, steel versus wood or steel versus concrete, applied to the same building, in order to understand the most eco-efficient solution, with the same mechanical performance [49, 50]. Or, in the design phase, the comparison of the environmental impacts allows to have a complete scenario of the performances between alternative technical solutions (envelope, surface finish, facade or roofing systems, thermal insulation, roof slab, and flooring), as well as esthetic, thermal, acoustic, fire resistance, etc., also those of environmental impact [51–60]. The constant underlying the comparative applications of LCA is the functional unit U.F.: it is important to compare different products, components, systems on the basis of an equal unit of performance, in order to make the relative results comparable (e.g. U.F. equal to 1 sq.m. of envelope surface, if I compare facade systems, U.F. equal to 1 m2 of usable floor area, if we compare quantities which, in order to be compared, must be normalized with respect to a common denominator).

There are more recent application studies of the LCA to the life cycle of the building, which begin to calculate the effects of the life span of the same and the durability of its parts in the life cycle, considering the impact related to the maintenance and replacement of parties [61, 62]. Other studies focus on concepts of dynamic LCA (dynamic LCA), i.e. they evaluate the building's performance considering the temporal variations in the internal environment and the external conditions during the operational life of a building, incorporating the possibility of quickly updating the LCA results on the basis of changes to the project or on the variation of the functioning of the building (dynamic modeling scenarios) [63, 64].

Compared to the different architectural scales, there are different attitudes in the LCA application strategies regarding the consideration of all or only some of the synthetic environmental indicators: some applications adopt the strategy of simplification by carrying out an LCA evaluation which verifies only the energy consumption (indicator of Embodied Energy) and the equivalent carbon dioxide emissions (global warming potential indicator) [65–68], with the consequent facilitation in the immediate comparison of the results between the phases of the life cycle, as well as a dissemination of the final values more user-friendly, since energy savings and CO_2eq. emissions are more commonly known and widespread concepts with respect to the environmental problems of water and soil acidification, rather than SO_2eq. emissions for the depletion of the ozone layer.

Certainly, there are still advances to be pursued in the transfer of this methodology to the architecture sector, harmonizations in procedures, in order to make the results of similar studies, carried out in different research or application contexts, much more comparable. It is necessary to make designers more aware of the assessment of the environmental problems generated by the design and construction act and to make them understand how, once again, environmental issues cannot be simplified to avoid complexity or manipulated to obtain brands or labels, but they must be taken seriously and fully understood. In any case, it is understandable how it is not easy from the LCA application theory to be able to match completeness and correctness in the eco-efficiency of the solutions adopted in a building and for all phases of the life cycle. Each situation is singular and unique, linked to a physical, territorial, and social context, and it is possible to calibrate the architectural and constructive choice on this, not forgetting the verification of the environmental impacts, perhaps not for all phases of the life cycle, but adopting design and construction strategies that we have in mind the building and the possible scenarios in the different phases.

6. Conclusions

The world of academic research has the task of focusing on increasingly precise answers so that environmental protection is not just a slogan. As Gianfranco Bologna states about the sustainable development formula: "Keeping the conceptual contours of this formula vague, albeit extremely difficult, and not comparing the real problems that derive from the implementation of sustainability in our development processes means proceeding with an unjustified action from a scientific point of view and incorrect from a social, economic, and political point of view" [69]. But university research also has the task of strenuously defending a vision of the relationship between design and environmental sustainability that knows how to understand all the problematic wealth that characterizes it, opposing the reductive simplifications that partisan interests often impose.

Author details

Carol Monticelli
Architecture, Built Environment and Construction Engineering Department, Textiles Hub - Interdepartmental Laboratory, Politecnico di Milano, Milano, Italy

*Address all correspondence to: carol.monticelli@polimi.it

References

[1] Aa. Vv. Libro bianco "Energia Ambiente Edificio". Ore, Milano: Il Sole 24; 2004

[2] Bistagnino L, Casati B, Jachia E. Definizione di progettazione ambientale ecosostenibile. In: Gamba G, Martinetti G, editors. Dizionario dell'ambiente. Torino: UTET; 2003

[3] Bell S, Madison. Lavoisier in the year one: The birth of a new science in an age of revolution. In: Atlas Books. W.W. Norton; 2005

[4] Tam V, Le K. Sustainable construction technologies life-cycle assessment. Oxford: Butterworth-Heinemann; 2019

[5] Bendewald M, Olgyay V, Yeang K. Green footstep a tool for evaluating a building's life-cycle carbon footprint and informing carbon decisions during the building design process. Architectural Design - Special Issue: Territory: Architecture Beyond Environment. 2010;**80**(3) John Wiley & Sons:126-129

[6] Blengini GA, Di Carlo T. The changing role of life cycle phases, subsystems and materials in the LCA of low energy buildings. Energy and Buildings. 2010;**42**:869-880

[7] Niklaus K, Klingele M, Heitz S, Hermann M, Koch M. Simulation of energy. 1997

[8] Blengini GA. Life cycle of buildings, demolition and recycling potential: A case study in Turin, Italy. Building and Environment. 2009;**44**:319-330

[9] Buth C, Achard G, Le Teno JF, Chevalier JL. Integration of the recycling processes to the life cycle analysis of construction products. Resources, Conservation and Recycling. 1997;**20**:227-243

[10] Schuurmans-Stehmann AM. Environmental life cycle analysis of construction products with and without recycling. In: Aalbers ThG, van der Sloot HA, Goumans JJJM, (editors). Environmental Aspects of Construction with Waste Materials. 1994. pp. 709-718

[11] Thormark C. A low energy building in a life cycle—Its embodied energy, energy need for operation and recycling potential. Building and Environment. 2002;**37**:429-435

[12] Alting DL, Jøgensen DJ. The life cycle concept as a basis for sustainable industrial production. CIRP Annals - Manufacturing Technology. 1993;**42**(1):163-167

[13] Alting DL, Legarth JB. Life cycle engineering and design. CIRP Annals - Manufacturing Technology. 1995;**44**(2):569-580

[14] Goggin PA. An appraisal of ecolabelling from a design perspective. Design Studies. 1994;**15**(4):459-477

[15] Holloway L, Clegg D, Tranter I, Cockerham G. Incorporating environmental principles into the design process. Materials & Design. 1994;**15**(5):259-267

[16] Matthews HS, Mcmichael F, Lave L, Maclean H. Life cycle analysis as a tool for product design. In: Encyclopaedia of Materials. Oxford U.K: Science and Technology, Elsevier Science Ltd.; 2001

[17] Erlandsson M, Borg M. Generic LCA-methodology applicable for buildings,

constructions and operation services—Today practice and development needs. Building and Environment. 2003;**38**:919-938

[18] Lee K, Tae S, Shin S. Development of a life cycle assessment program for building (SUSB-LCA) in South Korea. Renewable and Sustainable Energy Reviews. 2009;**13**:1994-2002

[19] Li Z. A new life cycle impact assessment approach for buildings. Building and Environment. 2006;**41**:1414-1422

[20] Mahdavi A, RIES R. Towards computational eco-analysis of building designs. Computers & Structures. 1998;**76**:375-387

[21] Malmqvist T et al. Life cycle assessment in buildings: The ENSLIC simplified method and guidelines. Energy. 2011;**36**:1900-1907

[22] Millet D, Bistagnino L, Lanzavecchia C, Camous R, Poldma T. Does the potential of the use of LCA match the design team needs? Journal of Cleaner Production. 2007;**15**:335-346

[23] Polster B et al. Evaluation of the environmental quality of buildings towards a more environmentally conscious design. Solar Energy. 1996;**57**(3):219-230

[24] Verbeeck G, Hens H. Life cycle inventory of buildings: A calculation method. Building and Environment. 2010;**45**:1037-1041

[25] Zhang Z, Wua X, Yanga X, Zhub Y. BEPAS—A life cycle building environmental performance assessment model. Building and Environment. 2006;**41**:669-675

[26] Abel CA, Edwards KL, Ashby MF. Materials, processing and the environment in engineering design: The issues. Materials & Design. 1994;**15**(4):179-193

[27] Alcorn A. Embodied Energy Coefficients of Building Materials. New Zealand: Centre for Building Performance Research, Victoria University of Wellington; 1998

[28] Bovea MD, Gallardo A. The influence of impact assessment methods on materials selection for eco-design. Materials and Design. 2004;**27**:209-215

[29] Chevalier GL, Tfinot L. Requirements for an LCA-based model for the evaluation of the environmental quality of building products. Building and Environment. 1996;**31**(5):487-491

[30] Jöhsson A. Tools and methods for environmental assessment of building products-methodological analysis of six selected approaches. Building and Environment. 2000;**35**:223-238

[31] Ortiz O et al. Sustainability based on LCM of residential dwellings: A case study in Catalonia, Spain. Building and Environment. 2009a;**44**:584-594

[32] Asif M, Muneer T, Kelley R. Life cycle assessment: A case study of a dwelling home in Scotland. Building and Environment. 2007;**42**:1391-1394

[33] Blengini GA, Di Carlo T. Energy-saving policies and low-energy residential buildings: An LCA case study to support d decision makers in Piedmont (Italy). International Journal of Life Cycle Assessment. 2010b;**15**:652-665

[34] Kofoworola OF, Shabbir HG. Environmental life cycle assessment of a commercial office building in Thailand. International Journal of Life Cycle Assessment. 2008;**13**:498-451

[35] Ortiz O, Castells F, Sonnemann G. Sustainability in the construction

industry: A review of recent developments based on LCA. Construction and Building Materials. 2009b;**23**:28-39

[36] Haapio A, Viitaniemi P. Environmental effect of structural solutions and building materials to a building. Environmental Impact Assessment Review. 2008;**28**:587-600

[37] Chan Y, Ries RJ, Wang Y. The embodied energy and environmental emissions of construction projects in China: An economic input–output LCA model. Energy Policy. 2010;**38**:6597-6603

[38] Cuéllar-Franca RM, Azapagic A. Environmental impacts of the UK residential sector: Life cycle assessment of houses. Building and Environment. 2012;**54**:86-99

[39] Ortiz-Rodríguez O, Castells F, Sonnemann G. Life cycle assessment of two dwellings: One in Spain, a developed country, and one in Colombia, a country under development. Science of the Total Environment. 2010;**408**:2435-2443

[40] Peuportier BLP. Life cycle assessment applied to the comparative evaluation of single-family houses in the French context. Energy and Buildings. 2001;**33**:443-450

[41] Rossi B, Marique AF, Reiter S. Life-cycle assessment of residential buildings in three different European locations, case study. Building and Environment. 2012;**51**:402-407

[42] Thiers S, Peuportier B. Energy and environmental assessment of two high energy performance residential buildings. Building and Environment. 2012;**51**:276-284

[43] Perez Fernandez N. The Influence of Construction Materials on Life-Cycle Energy Use and Carbon Dioxide Emissions of Medium Size Commercial Buildings, Master Degree in Building Science. New Zealand: School of Architecture, Victoria University of Wellington; 2008

[44] Wu HJ et al. Life cycle energy consumption and CO2 emission of an office building in China. International Journal of Life Cycle Assessment. 2012;**17**:105-118

[45] Varun et al. Life cycle environmental assessment of an educational building in northern India: A case study. Sustainable Cities and Society. 2012;**4**:22-28

[46] Ardente et al. Energy and environmental benefits in public buildings as a result of retrofit actions. Renewable and Sustainable Energy Reviews. 2011;**15**(1):460-470

[47] Iyer-Raniga U, Wong JP. Evaluation of whole life cycle assessment for heritage buildings in Australia. Building and Environment. 2012;**47**:138-149

[48] Myer A, Chaffee C. Life-cycle analysis for design of the Sydney Olympic Stadium. Renewable Energy. 1997;**10**(213):169-172

[49] Eaton JK, Amato A. A comparative life cycle assessment of steel and concrete framed office buildings. Journal of Constructional Steel Research. 1998;**46**:286-287

[50] Lenzen M, Treloar G. Embodied energy in buildings: Wood versus concrete - reply to Börjesson and Gustavsson. Energy Policy. 2002;**30**:249-255

[51] Azari-Na R, Kim YW. Comparative assessment of life cycle impacts of curtain wall mullions. Building and Environment. 2012;**48**:135-145

[52] Citherlet S, Di Guglielmo F, Gay JB. Window and advanced glazing systems life cycle assessment. Energy and Buildings. 2000;**32**:225-234

[53] Kim KH. A comparative life cycle assessment of a transparent composite façade system and a glass curtain wall system. Energy and Buildings. 2011;**43**:3436-3445

[54] Kosareo L, Ries R. Comparative environmental life cycle assessment of green roof. Building and Environment. 2007;**42**:2606-2613

[55] Monteiro H, Freire F. Life-cycle assessment of a house with alternative exterior walls: Comparison of three impact assessment methods. Energy and Buildings. 2012;**47**:572-583

[56] Nebel B, Zimmer B, Wegener G. Life cycle assessment of wood floor coverings. A representative study for the German flooring industry. International Journal of Life Cycle Assessment. 2006;**11**(3):172-182

[57] Nicoletti G et al. Comparative life cycle assessment of flooring materials: Ceramic versus marble tiles. Journal of Cleaner Production. 2002;**10**:283-296

[58] Ottele M et al. Comparative life cycle analysis for green façades and living wall systems. Energy and Buildings. 2011;**43**:3419-3429

[59] Petersen AK, Solberg B. Environmental and economic impacts of substitution between wood products and alternative materials: A review of micro-level analyses from Norway and Sweden. Forest Policy and Economics. 2005;**7**:249-259

[60] Potting J, Block K. Life-cycle assessment of four types of floors. Journal of Cleaner Production. 1995;**3**(4):201-213

[61] Aktar CB, Bilec MM. Impact of lifetime on US residential building LCA results. International Journal of Life Cycle Assessment. 2012;**17**:337-349

[62] Blom I, Itard L, Meijer A. LCA-based environmental assessment of the use and maintenance of heating and ventilation systems in Dutch dwellings. Building and Environment. 2010;**45**:2362-2372

[63] Collinge WO et al. Enabling dynamic life cycle assessment of buildings with wireless sensor networks. In: IEEE International Symposium on Sustainable Systems and Technology (ISSST). Chicago, IL, USA: Maggio; 2011. pp. 16-18

[64] Pehnt M. Dynamic life cycle assessment (LCA) of renewable energy technologies. Renewable Energy. 2006;**31**:55-71

[65] Asdrubali F, Baldinelli G, Battisti M, Baldassarri C. Analisi ed ottimizzazione energetico-ambientale di un edificio mediante la valutazione del ciclo di vita (LCA). In: Proceedings of the Eighth Natioanl COnference CIRIAF - Sviluppo Sostenibile, Tutela dell'Ambiente e Della Salute Umana, Perugia, 4/5 Aprile. Perugia: Morlacchi Editore; 2008

[66] Koroneos C, Kottas G. Energy consumption modeling analysis and environmental impact assessment of model house in Thessaloniki—Greece. Building and Environment. 2005;**42**:122-138

[67] Lin SL. LCA-based energy evaluating with application to school buildings in Taiwan. In: Proceedings of Design 2003 - Third International Symposium on Environmentally Conscious Design and Inverse Manufacturing. Tokyo, Japan; 2003. Available from: https://www.computer.org/csdl/proceedings-article/ecodim/2003/01322703/12OmNxH9X7s

[68] Monahan J, Powell JC. An embodied carbon and energy analysis of modern methods of construction in housing: A case study using a lifecycle assessment

framework. Energy and Buildings. 2011;**43**:179-188

[69] Wang X, Ramakrishnan S. Environmental sustainability in building design and construction. Geneve, Switzerland: Springer Cham; 2022

Chapter 2

Life Cycle Assessment of Buildings: An End-of-Life Perspective

Augustine Blay-Armah, Ali Bahadori-Jahromi, Golnaz Mohebbi and Anastasia Mylona

Abstract

Building demolition waste represents a huge environmental challenge worldwide. The environmental implications are not only associated with volume, but also with carbon embodied in the waste. These adverse environmental impacts associated with the generated waste can be minimised through appropriate waste treatment strategies. This chapter evaluates the various stages of the life cycle of demolished waste materials, the potential carbon emission reduction associated with different demolished wastes and waste treatment strategy options. An assessment framework was developed and exemplified by a case study of a supermarket building. The results showed that the processing or treatment stage generate the largest amount of carbon emission (81%) in the life cycle of demolished waste materials, whilst the transportation stage contributed the least (1%). It was further found that steel waste recycling has the greatest environmental benefits (more than 90%) compared to concrete (less than 1%). Additionally, the study revealed that landfilling waste generated the largest amount of carbon emissions compared to recycling. The findings can contribute to mitigating the environmental building demolition projects. Furthermore, the detailed assessment approach provides theoretical and methodological guidance which can be adopted to guide the quantitative analysis of other types of demolition projects globally.

Keywords: embodied carbon emissions, end-of-life, building waste materials, life cycle assessment, recycling, landfilling

1. Introduction

The construction sector is a mainstay of many economies around the world. It has inherent value through the creation of distinctive economic and social products. However, the sector also generates a huge impact on the environment, which raises sustainability concerns. One of the environmental concerns is the generation of large volumes of construction and demolition (C&D) waste, along with the carbon embodied in them. For example, the industry is responsible for nearly 50% of the solid waste sent to landfills [1]. In the European Union (EU), C&D waste is around 20–30% (Ding, 2018). Waste Statistics compiled by Defra [2] indicate that in 2016, 63% of the total waste stream in England (189 million tonnes) was attributed to construction, demolition and excavation waste. Of this figure, an estimated 50% was attributed to C&D waste. C&D waste is described as a mixture of different waste streams, including inert waste, non-hazardous waste and hazardous waste, generated from construction, renovation, and demolition activities of buildings, roads, bridges and other structures [3]. As a result of its impact on the environment, the EU has classified C&D waste as a priority for its members to reduce [4].

In contrast with construction projects, however, demolition projects generate a greater volume of waste [5]. Consequently, the environmental concern of demolition waste does not only relate to the amount generated, but also its treatment. The commonly used treatment methods in dealing with demolition waste include reuse, recycling and landfill [6, 7]. These treatment methods require waste collection, sorting, transportation, recycling and final disposal. These treatment processes are referred to as the demolition waste life cycle [7–9]. Throughout the steps of treating demolished waste, a significant amount of carbon emissions is emitted as a result of energy utilisation associated with transportation and machine operations [7, 10, 11]. Nevertheless, recycling as an end-of-life treatment strategy bears positive and negative environmental impacts [12], since recycling demolished waste can reduce the extraction of virgin building materials [13]. Since the increase in end-of-life waste considerably impacts the overall construction industry's carbon emissions performance, the industry and practitioners need a low-carbon emission treatment strategy for demolished waste. Therefore, the evaluation of environmental effects associated with end-of-life waste management along with the selection of a low-carbon emission management approach is the response of the building and construction sector to environmental challenges. This evaluation and selection should start with an appropriate quantification method for the life cycle carbon emission of the building demolition waste [4, 14].

Life cycle assessment (LCA) is a widely recognised tool used in the evaluation of the environmental performance of a product or procedure over its entire life cycle [15]. Many previous studies relating to a building's life cycle considered one or some specific phases of the life cycle of a building such as material manufacture, construction or use [16, 17]. Other researchers focussed on the assessment of the entire life cycle of a building [18, 19]. Few studies, however, place emphasis on end-of-life carbon emission assessment of the life cycle of a building [20–22]. The quantification of carbon emissions resulting from building demolition waste treatment is mostly ignored [7, 20, 23]. For a clear understanding of the life cycle carbon emission associated with building demolition waste, an in-depth consideration of the processes and activities involved in demolition and treatment of waste is needed.

One of the challenges of conducting an LCA is accurate data acquisition. However, the use of building information modelling (BIM) directly provides data including geometric information, physical attributes and material quantities [24, 25]. The integration of LCA and BIM not only overcomes the need to enter information manually but also combines the strengths of both tools [26, 27]. Thus, BIM provides efficient means of acquiring essential data for carrying out life cycle assessment of buildings, while streamlining the process of data collection [28, 29]. Yet, few studies adopt a BIM-LCA integrated approach in the evaluation of end-of-life carbon emissions [7]. Meanwhile, various past studies have suggested that the building and construction sector can play a vital role in the mitigation of climate change by properly controlling and minimising carbon emissions from construction and demolition activities [30, 31].

The chapter aims to propose an integrated analytical framework based on the LCA model for assessing the impact of the life cycle stages of demolished waste materials, waste material type and waste treatment options on carbon emission reduction. In contrast with other studies, this chapter contributes to mitigating the environmental impact of a demolished supermarket building and exemplifies this with a case study. In addition, it contributes to the theoretical frameworks for quantifying the environmental impact of demolished waste materials by clearly addressing the following questions: (i) "which stage of the life cycle demolished waste critically influence carbon emissions reduction?" (ii) "What type of demolished waste material greatly impacts end-of-life carbon emission reduction?" (iii) "which waste treatment strategy significantly affect end-of-life carbon emissions reduction?" Comprehensive and detailed analyses were performed to better understand the research trends and knowledge gaps in this discipline.

2. Materials and methods

2.1 Case study

This research employed a case to conduct detailed calculations of carbon emission during the end-of-life. A case study is recognised to be appropriate in investigating complex research particularly, where there is a lack of data available to understand the effect of demolished building waste and the treatment strategies on carbon emissions [10]. The selected case study was a current UK supermarket building. The case building was a single-storey with an average area of 2500 m^2. Autodesk® Revit® BIM software was used to provide the data on demolition waste generation. Design drawings were obtained and validated with a site survey. The case building simulation is shown in **Figure 1**. The height of the front elevation was 7.02 m while the back was 5.10 m.

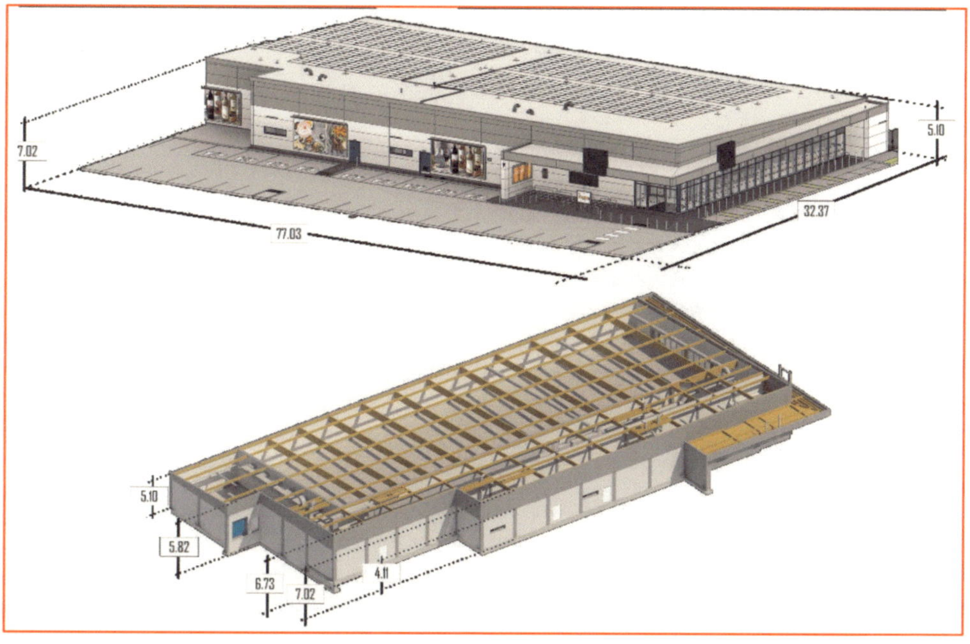

Figure 1.
The simulated model of the case building.

Waste material type	Building component	Weight (kg)
	Category A	
Aluminium	Windows; Doors; Roof; Curtain walls	9618.60
Concrete		1,881,559.12
Steel	Iron pieces; Steel in concrete	240,875.19
Plastic	Pipes and other plastic materials	135.91
Glass	Windows; Doors; Curtain walls	7190.75
Timber	Structural columns; Roof frames	66,921.64
	Category B	
Gypsum	Walls; Ceilings	46,746.45
Mortar	Wall plaster	2765.08
Tiles	Floor; Ceiling	61,639.23
Mixed materials		44,622.31
Total		2,362,074.29

Table 1.
Inventory of main waste materials in the case building.

The structural form determines the main materials. The main materials in the case building are displayed in **Table 1** along with the quantities. The waste materials were derived from two categories. The waste materials in category **A** are considered waste with a high recyclable value. Category **B**, on the other hand, is considered waste with a very low recyclable value and is therefore landfilled. This is because large-scale demolition is usually carried out using mechanised techniques. Consequently, the generated demolished waste is in small volumes, difficult to sort and is generally generated in a mixed form [32].

2.2 Carbon emission factors of the main waste materials and end-of-life stages

The life cycle of demolished waste materials involved various stages and a series of processes (see Section 2.3.3 for a full explanation). Carbon emission factors (CEFs) are vitally important as they affect the accuracy of the life cycle calculation results. CEFs can be derived from numerous sources. More localised CEFs enhance the accuracy of the assessment results [33]. Consequently, the choice CEFs was based on the principle of regional priority. CEFs of the main waste materials are listed in **Table 2**.

2.3 Life cycle assessment

The life cycle of waste materials involves various processes and activities. In this study, the assessment used is consistent with the four ISO standards for LCA: definition of scope and goal; life cycle inventory (LCI) which quantifies the inputs; inventory analysis (LCIA) which converts the inputs to emissions; and interpretation of results.

Based on the above breakdowns, the LCA estimation model was developed to evaluate the life cycle carbon emission of demolished waste materials. To generate

Stages	Carbon emission factor ($kgCO_2eq.$)
Demolition & deconstruction stage	
Demolishing by machine	3.400[b,c]
Transportation stage	
Transporting waste to processing plant & disposal site:	
Aluminium	1.31E-02[a]
Concrete, steel, plastics, glass, timber, mortar & mixed materials	0.1065[b,c]
Tiles	1.01E-1[a]
Processing of waste – recycling	
Aluminium	1.07E-02[a]
Steel, plastics, glass & concrete	0.013[b,c]
Timber	1.67[b,c]
Roof	9.54E+01[a]
Disposal – Landfill	
Aluminium	0.00E+01[a]
Concrete, steel, plastics, glass, mortar & mixed materials	0.013[b,c]
Timber	2.15[b,c]
Tiles	4.63E+01[a]
Material recovery	
Aluminium	−3.98[a]
Concrete	−0.000989[d]
Steel	−1.6[b,c]
Timber	−0.524[b,c]
Roof	−17.43[a]

[a]*Environmental Product Declaration (EPD).*[b]*Royal Institute of Chartered Surveyors (RICS) [34]*[c]*The Institute of Structural Engineers (IStructE) [35]*[d]*The Department for Business, Energy and Industrial Strategy (BEIS) [36].*

Table 2.
Waste materials and carbon emission factors.

data for the estimation, BIM was used, while data from other sources were used to complement the estimation.

2.3.1 Scope, goal and system boundaries definitions

This LCA examines the carbon emissions of demolished building waste materials under two end-of-life treatment strategies (see Section 2.3.4). Data was taken from a UK supermarket building. As noted above, an assessment framework that incorporates BIM with an LCA was used to provide data on demolition waste generation. The assessment framework comprises various elements as illustrated in **Figure 2**. The scope and goal phase covers all activities and resources involved in the process of demolished waste from generation to final disposal.

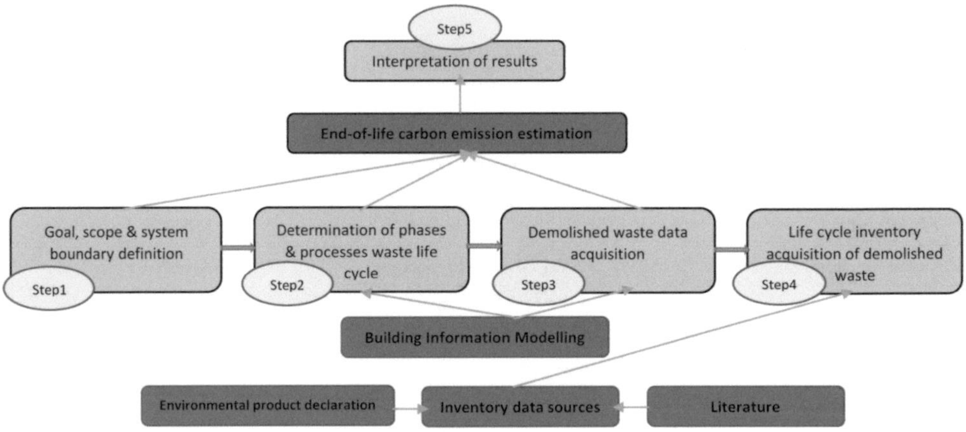

Figure 2.
Framework of carbon emission assessment of demolished waste [7].

In LCA, functional units are used to ensure like-to-like comparisons. In this study, the functional unit of demolished waste considers two variables – materials weight (kg) and carbon emission (kgCO_2eq). In order to scale up the results to any weight of demolished waste material, the functional unit will consider 1 kg of waste materials. The functional unit is therefore kgCO_2eq of per 1 kg demolished waste.

2.3.2 Life cycle inventory

The main type of life cycle inventory (LCI) and data used was the process LCI (primary and secondary environmental data). The process LCI was used to systematically quantify the physical inputs and outputs of the waste materials within the process LCA system boundary. The process LCI of each component and activity was derived using the breakdown approach, which gives carbon emissions per kg of waste material generated. The LCA quantification formulas were developed to estimate the life cycle carbon emission during the end-of-life (see **Figure 2**). As stated earlier, the LCA was integrated with BIM to provide data imported into the calculation of end-of-life carbon emissions. During these end-of-life activities and processes, records of energy consumption by machines were sought through multiple data sources including EPDs from manufacturers/suppliers and site surveys. To complement the robustness of these data, additional carbon emission factors for each phase and activity were gathered from other literature. Where data was not available from EPD and recognised eco-data source the mean value of the other literature searches was used.

2.3.3 Life cycle impact assessment of demolished building material

As noted in Section 2.1.2, the life cycle impact assessment (LCIA) approach employed in this study was the process-based LCA inventories (where the physical flow of all aspects of building materials can be identified and traced) to establish the carbon emission embodied in building demolished waste. As an LCA technique, the process-based has the strength to reveal carbon emissions from the specific demolition process and activity, along with its accuracy and detailed processes [17, 37, 38]. The rationale of this method is straightforward and clear, carbon emissions from individual activities can be estimated and analysed separately [17]. This method is frequently adopted in the quantification of carbon emissions of construction processes [17, 39, 40]. Finally, the results of the LCIA were then analysed and the conclusions were drawn.

Meanwhile, there are four stages of the life cycle the waste materials and a series of activities are involved. The analysis of these activities is fundamental to identifying carbon emission factors (CEFs). The first stage covers all the processes in the demolition of the building at the end of its useful life. During the demolition, several machines can be used and energy/fuel consumed through the use of these machines or equipment as well as related emissions serve as a source of CEF. Carbon emissions at this phase also include the projected operating time for machines or equipment used in carrying out the demolition of the building multiplied by the average electric power used and/or fuel per unit of time and the related carbon intensity per litre of fuel used. The second stage covers the transportation of the demolished waste materials to treatment plants, recycling plants or landfill sites. CEFs are also derived from the environmental impacts associated with these activities. The third stage covers all the processes in the waste treatment plant, while the fourth and final stage covers the processes associated with the final disposal of demolished building materials.

The conceptual LCA framework focuses on the demolished building materials for which waste treatment is expected, and therefore, the environmental impacts were calculated. However, two aspects of carbon emission are associated with recycling waste materials - the adverse environmental effects and the environmental benefits [7]. The net environmental impact is equal to the difference between the impacts due to the recycling process that replaces the production of virgin materials and the impacts due to the production of the avoided virgin material. The net benefits associated with material replacement and energy consumption, or carbon emission is the difference between the input and output of the secondary material.

Using life cycle inventories, the process LCA for the use of machine/equipment can be defined by Eq. (1) as:

$$EC_{equip} = \sum EQi * EQFi * EQECi \tag{1}$$

Where:

EC_{equip} refers to carbon emission associated with plant or equipment used in dismantling or demolishing a building at the end-of-life ($kgCO_2eq$); EQ_i refers to the number of hours plant/equipment $_i$ is used for the dismantling or demolition process (hour); EQF_i refers to the type of fuel used by the demolition plant/equipment $_i$ (kWh or litre per hour); and $EQEC_i$ refers to carbon intensity per unit consumption of fuel $_i$ ($kgCO_2eq$ per litre).

Carbon emission is also calculated for waste generation during the demolition of the building. It is assumed that waste from the demolished building during the end-of-life of the case building is equal to the mass of material in the constructed building excluding the waste factor and has the same building component category breakdown. Consequently, the process LCA of building demolition can be represented by Eq. (2) as:

$$EC_{struct} = \sum Si * SCEFi \tag{2}$$

Where:

EC_{struct} refers to carbon emission associated with the demolished building; S_i refers to the quantity of material $_i$ resulting from the demolished structure or building (m^2, m^3 or kg); and $SCEF_i$ denotes the carbon emission coefficient per unit of material $_i$ ($kgCO_2eq$ per kg, m^3 or m^2).

Using life cycle inventories, the process LCA for transporting demolished materials can be defined by Eq. (3) as:

$$EC_{transp} = \sum TDi * TLi * TFi * TCEFi \quad (3)$$

Where:

TD_i denotes the total distance covered for material $_i$ (km); TL_i refers to the number of loads of trucks for the transportation of material $_i$ (No.); TFi represents the fuel used per load of truck (litre per km); and $TECF_i$ refers to the carbon emission coefficient per fuel unit used $_i$ (kgCO_2eq per litre).

In this study, two waste treatment approaches - recycling and landfilling were assumed. As noted above, recycling demolished waste materials has both adverse environmental impacts and environmental benefits. Therefore, the environmental benefits of substituting virgin materials with recycled (secondary) materials are subtracted. Subsequently, the process LCA for recycling demolition waste can be defined by Eq. (4) as:

$$EC_{rec} = \sum EC_{rec-qe}i - EC_{rec-(-ben)}i \quad (4)$$

Where:

EC_{rec} is the carbon emission from the recycling plant (kgCO_2eq.); $EC_{rec\text{-}qe}$ is the emission resulting from machine operation during recycling (kgCO_2eq); and $EC_{rec\text{-}(-ben)}$ is the carbon emission reduction through the replacement of raw materials (kgCO_2eq).

Accordingly, using life cycle inventories, the process LCA for the total carbon emissions of the demolished waste over the life cycle for recycling and landfill treatment options can be represented by Eq. (5) and (6) respectively.

$$EC_{TOTALREC} = \sum EC_{de} + EC_{tp} + EC_{pr} \quad (5)$$

$$EC_{TOTALLAN} = \sum EC_{de} + EC_{tp} + EC_{dp} \quad (6)$$

Where:

$EC_{TOTALREC}$ and $EC_{TOTALLAN}$ refer to the total carbon emission of the life cycle of building demolition waste for recycling and landfilling respectively (kgCO_2eq); EC_{de} is the carbon emission at the demolition phase (kgCO_2eq); EC_{tp} is the carbon emission during transportation phase (kgCO_2eq); and EC_{pr} refers to the carbon emission during recycling (kg CO_2eq.), while EC_{dp} is the carbon emission during disposal.

Results analysis is a key aspect of a life cycle assessment study. Therefore, through the scenario analysis, the stage of the end-of-life with greater carbon emission can be identified. Also, the type of waste material and treatment strategy with the largest carbon emission potential can be identified. Hence, low-carbon waste materials can be proposed to manage the end-of-life carbon emission and associated substantial amounts of building waste. Accordingly, the process LCA for the comparison waste can be defined by Eq. (7) as:

$$P_{eol} = B_{eol} / \sum B_{eol} \quad (7)$$

Where:

P_{eol} is the proportion of carbon emission from a stage of demolition waste life cycle, treatment strategy and type of waste material the case building (%).

B_{eol} is the total carbon emission from the case building (kgCO_2eq).

2.3.4 End-of-life scenarios and assumptions

In this study, two waste treatment options were considered. Based on the recovery rates of the UK from localised literature and other sources, the percentage of each material was determined. **Table 3** shows the assumed end-of-life treatment options for the waste materials along with the percentages A heavy-duty diesel truck (17 tonnes load) was assumed as a transportation mode for the demolished waste materials [34, 35]. In addition, a maximum distance of 50 km by road for both treatment options was assumed.

3. Results

3.1 Carbon emission impact of life cycle stages of demolished waste material

According to the analytical assessment model, the total carbon emission of different stages in the lifecycle of the waste materials was calculated (see **Table 4**). The value of the treatment stage was the largest representing about 81% of the total end-of-life carbon emission. This includes the environmental impact of input/output of treating and recycling demolished waste, carbon emission reduction of waste replacement as well as landfilling unrecyclable waste. The carbon emission values of demolition and transportation stages accounted for 18% and 1% respectively. The carbon emission of the treatment stage is influenced by different carbon emission values compared to the demolition stage (see **Table 2**). Despite being the major carbon emission contributor, if recycling is selected, where possible, for waste treatment, the reuse of recycled materials could result in environmental benefits. This suggests that the choice of waste material treatment option should be given priority in order to reduce carbon embodied in them.

Waste Material	Demolition/Dismantling	Treatment Option		Weight	
		Recycle (%)	Landfill (%)	Recycle (kg)	Landfill (kg)
Aluminium	Demolition	92	8	8849.11	769.59
Concrete	Demolition	90	10	1,693,403.21	188,155.91
Steel	Demolition	92	8	221,605.17	19,270.02
Plastic	Demolition	50	50	67.95	67.95
Glass	Demolition	50	50	3595.38	3595.38
Insulation	Demolition	—	100		66,921.64
Timber	Demolition	55	45	25,710.55	21,035.90
Gypsum	Demolition	—	100		2765.08
Tiles	Demolition	—	100		61,639.23
Mortar	Demolition	—	100		2765.08
Mixed materials	Demolition	—	100		44,622.31
Total				1,953,231.37	411,608.00

Table 3.
End-of-life options for common building elements.

Stage	Carbon emission ($kgCO_2eq$)
Demolition	114,388.47
Transportation	9323.49
Treatment	530,322.71
Total	654,034.67

Table 4.
Carbon emission of life cycle stages of demolished waste materials.

Table 4 indicates that transportation is by far the least carbon emission end-of-life stage. This is because the distance of transporting waste materials to the processing plant or disposal site is located locally. This result emphasises the need for selecting local processing facilities as long distance defeats the goal of carbon emission reduction.

3.2 Carbon emission reduction potential of waste materials replacement

The total carbon emission reduction that can be achieved through replacement was −797,147.34 $kgCO_2eq$. Steel accounted for the majority of the environmental benefits and was much higher than other materials in the case building even though it represents only 10% of the total waste materials (see **Figure 3**). Aluminium was the second largest contributor, followed by timber and concrete. As illustrated in **Figure 3**, the environmental benefit of concrete contributes to as low as 0.16%, although it accounts for nearly 80% of the weight of all generated waste. This is because the value of the environmental benefit of concrete in terms of carbon emission reduction potential is much smaller than that of steel and aluminium. For example, the environmental benefit of recovering one kg of aluminium (in the roof) for reuse can contribute to 17.43 kg CO_2eq of carbon emission reduction, while this value is only 0.000989 for

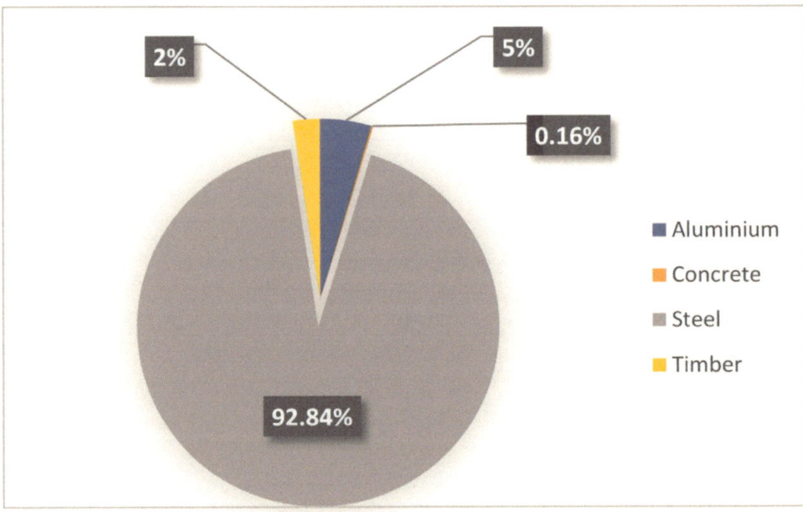

Figure 3.
Proportion of carbon emission reduction potential by waste materials.

recovering one kg of concrete. This result indicates that the recovery and the subsequent processing of metal should be given priority in terms of material potential to reduce carbon emissions during end-of-life.

3.3 Carbon emission of treatment options

As noted in Section 2.3.4, two waste treatment options (recycling and landfill) were considered to explore the best waste treatment strategy. The net environmental impacts or benefits due to recycling were also accounted for. **Figure 4** shows the contribution of each waste material to the two treatment options' carbon emissions. In all, 2,364,839.37 kg of waste was generated from the demolition of the case building. Out of this total, 83% were recycled accounting for 595,330.41 $kgCO_2eq$ of the overall carbon emissions, whereas landfilling waste contributed 150,945.83 $kgCO_2eq$. Recycling the waste materials, however, has huge environmental gains as indicated in **Figure 4**. The result reveals that recycling contributes a net environmental benefit of up to −201,816.93 $kgCO_2eq$ when the environmental gain is combined with the carbon emission. This suggests that the most significant end-of-life management option is recycling compared with landfilling demolished waste. Additionally, by comparing the two end-of-life management options, recycling contributed to a potential reduction of approximately 7% in overall carbon emissions.

4. Discussion of results

The management of the end-of-life of a building involves a series of processes and activities as well as diverse carbon-intensive waste materials. However, only limited studies have focused on combining the various stages of demolished waste materials, carbon emission reduction along with treatment strategies. This study aimed to develop an integrated analytical framework based on the LCA model to assess the impact of the life cycle stages of demolished waste materials on carbon emission in order to provide guidance for carbon emission reduction and raw materials conservation.

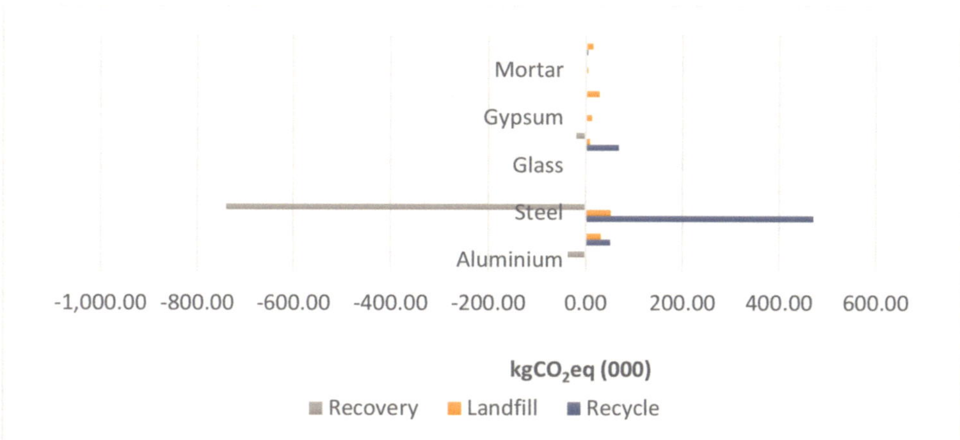

Figure 4.
Analysis of treatment options.

The results from the breakdown of the life cycle stages (demolition, transportation, processing and disposal) indicated that the processing or treatment stage generated the largest amount of carbon emission (81%) during end-of-life. On the other hand, the transportation of demolished waste material contributed the least (1%) to the total life cycle of carbon emission. The insignificant impact of the transportation stage on end-of-life carbon emissions has also been highlighted by previous studies. Coelho and de Brito [41, 42] assessed the carbon emission embodied in construction and demolition waste materials and suggested that the overall transportation distance should be always reduced because of the related energy consumption and carbon emissions.

As presented in the results section, carbon emission reduction can be achieved through the substitution effects of reusing recycled waste materials. While some past studies have indicated that the recycling of construction and demolition waste has environmental benefits due to the potential to replace virgin materials, the environmental performance of some demolished waste materials has been ignored. For example, a study to evaluate embodied carbon, [17] only considered the recycling of steel and aluminium. Similarly, a study to develop a model to evaluate the cradle-to-grave environmental impacts of a building in Italy, [43] only considered the recycling of steel and aggregate. The current study, however, considered at least four major waste materials. The analysis of the results revealed that steel has a significant impact on demolished waste life cycle carbon emission reduction. Despite representing only 10% of the total mass of generated waste materials, the result analysis indicates that steel has a carbon emission reduction potential of more than 90% of the case building. This result indicates that the recovery and the subsequent processing of metal should be given priority in terms of material potential to reduce carbon emissions during end-of-life.

Furthermore, by investigating the two waste treatment strategies (recycling and landfill) currently viable to the supermarket, this study revealed that landfilling generated the largest amount of carbon and the largest contributor to life cycle carbon emission during the end-of-life phase. In contrast, the analysis of the results emphasises that overall recycling building waste can lead to significant environmental benefits rather than adverse environmental impacts, particularly for materials with a high-value recyclable potential such as steel, aluminium and timber. This is due to the carbon emission reduction potential associated with material recovery. For instance, the results indicate that recycling instead of landfilling could achieve an overall 7% environmental benefit. The significant impact of recycling demolished waste materials has also been highlighted by previous studies. In a study to develop a model to evaluate the cradle-to-grave environmental impacts of a building in Italy, [43] stated that recycling steel and aggregate can lead to environmental gain. Similar findings were reported by [12, 41, 42], who found that recycling demolished waste materials could provide environmental benefits because of the potential to substitute raw materials. Conversely, [10] pointed out that the carbon emission associated with demolished waste materials can be considered lost if landfilled, since virgin materials would be required to replace them. Therefore, careful consideration should be given to the treatment strategies of demolished waste materials.

5. Conclusion

Building demolition waste represents a huge environmental challenge worldwide. The environmental implications are not only associated with volume, but also with carbon embodied in the waste. These adverse environmental impacts associated with the generated waste can be minimised through appropriate waste treatment strategies. This chapter evaluates the various stages of the life cycle of demolished waste materials, the potential carbon emission reduction associated with different demolished wastes and waste treatment strategy options. This was exemplified by a case study of a supermarket building. The analytical framework and the detailed method of quantifying the environmental impact have the potential to be adopted in other building demolition projects.

The results of this study show that the processing or treatment stage might generate the largest amount of carbon emission (81%) in the life cycle of demolished waste materials. In contrast, the transportation of stage contributed the least (1%) to the total life cycle of carbon emission.

Likewise, this study revealed that carbon emission reduction can be achieved through the substitution effects of reusing recycled waste materials. The analysis indicates there are environmental benefits to substituting virgin resources with recycled building-demolished waste, which compensates for the environmental impacts associated with the processing of waste materials. The environmental gain differs considerably from one waste material to another. For example, despite representing only 10% of the total mass of generated waste materials, steel has a carbon emission reduction potential of more than 90% of the case building. The recycling of metal (steel and aluminium) and timber-based materials should be given priority in terms of material potential to reduce carbon emissions during end-of-life.

Additionally, this study revealed that landfilling generated the largest amount of carbon and the largest contributor to life cycle carbon emission during the end-of-life phase. On the other hand, recycling demolished waste materials can lead to significant environmental, particularly for materials with a high-value recyclable potential such as steel, aluminium and timber. For instance, the results indicate that recycling over 80% of the total mass of generated waste materials could achieve an overall 7% environmental benefit.

This study offers some useful implications and guidance for designers, engineers and other stakeholders regarding the treatment of construction and demolition waste. For instance, where reuse is less viable, recycling waste should be considered an integral part of the demolished waste treatment strategy for each building's end-of-life project. The development of the waste treatment strategy should give major priority to metal waste such as steel and aluminium as well as wood-based materials because of their positive environmental performance during end-of-life treatment. Also, the findings reported in this study can contribute to mitigating the environmental impact of building demolition projects. Furthermore, the detailed assessment approach provides theoretical and methodological guidance which can be adopted to guide the quantitative analysis of other types of demolition projects globally. Finally, the findings complement the existing literature, which mainly addresses the environmental performances of demolished waste by means of the life cycle assessment methodology.

Additional information

Ali B-Jahromi: https://orcid.org/0000-0003-0405-7146

Author details

Augustine Blay-Armah*, Ali Bahadori-Jahromi*, Golnaz Mohebbi and Anastasia Mylona
Department of Civil Engineering and Built Environment, School of Computing and Engineering, University of West London, London, UK

*Address all correspondence to: augustine.blay-armah@uwl.ac.uk; ali.bahadori-jahromi@uwl.ac.uk

References

[1] Crowther P. Re-valuing construction materials and components through Design for Disassembly. In: Crocker R, Saint R, Chen G, Tong Y, editors. Unmaking Waste in Production and Consumption: Towards the Circular Economy. Bingley, UK: Emerald Publishing Limited; 2018. pp. 309-321. DOI: 10.1108/978-1-78714-619-820181024

[2] Defra. Resources and Waste Strategy, HM Government London, GOV.UK. 2018. Available from: https://www.gov.uk/government/publications/resources-and-waste-strategy-for-england [Accessed: December 20, 2022]

[3] European Commission. Directive 2008/98/EC of the European Parliament and of the Council on waste. 2008. Available from: https://eur-lex.europa.eu/legal-content/EN/ALL/?uri=celex%3A32008L0098 [Accessed: December 18, 2022]

[4] Gálvez-Martos J-L, Styles D, Schoenberger H, Zeschmar-Lahl B. Construction and demolition waste best management practice in Europe. Resources, Conservation and Recycling. 2018;**136**:166-178. DOI: 10.1016/j.resconrec.2018.04.016

[5] Duan H, Li J. Construction and demolition waste management: China's lessons. Waste Management & Research: The Journal for a Sustainable Circular Economy. 2016; **34**(5):397-398. DOI: 10.1177/0734242X16647603

[6] Tam V, Lu W. Construction waste management profiles, practices, and performance: A cross-jurisdictional analysis in four countries. Sustainability. 2016;**8**(2):190. DOI: 10.3390/su8020190

[7] Wang J, Wu H, Duan H, Zillante G, Zuo J, Yuan H. Combining life cycle assessment and building information modelling to account for carbon emission of building demolition waste: A case study. Journal of Cleaner Production. 2018;**172**:3154-3166. DOI: 10.1016/j.jclepro.2017.11.087

[8] Dahlbo H, Bachér J, Lähtinen K, Jouttijärvi T, Suoheimo P, Mattila T, et al. Construction and demolition waste management – A holistic evaluation of environmental performance. Journal of Cleaner Production. 2015;**107**:333-341. DOI: 10.1016/j.jclepro.2015.02.073

[9] Ortiz O, Pasqualino JC, Castells F. Environmental performance of construction waste: Comparing three scenarios from a case study in Catalonia, Spain. Waste Management. 2010;**30**(4): 646-654. DOI: 10.1016/j.wasman.2009.11.013

[10] Ding GKC. Embodied carbon in construction, maintenance and demolition in buildings. In: Pomponi F, De Wolf C, Moncaster A, editors. Embodied Carbon in Buildings: Measurement, Management, and Mitigation. 1st ed. 2018. Cham: Springer International Publishing; p. 158–178. doi: 10.1007/978-3-319-72796-7

[11] Kucukvar M, Egilmez G, Tatari O. Life cycle assessment and optimization-based decision analysis of construction waste recycling for a LEED-certified university building. Sustainability. 2016; **8**(1):89. DOI: 10.3390/su8010089

[12] Silva RV, de Brito J, Dhir RK. Availability and processing of recycled aggregates within the construction and demolition supply chain: A review.

Journal of Cleaner Production. 2017;**143**: 598-614. DOI: 10.1016/j.jclepro.2016.12.070

[13] Hossain MU, Wu Z, Poon CS. Comparative environmental evaluation of construction waste management through different waste sorting systems in Hong Kong. Waste Management. 2017;**69**:325-335. DOI: 10.1016/j.wasman.2017.07.043

[14] Mastrucci A, Marvuglia A, Popovici E, Leopold U, Benetto E. Geospatial characterization of building material stocks for the life cycle assessment of end-of-life scenarios at the urban scale. Resources, Conservation and Recycling. 2017;**123**:54-66. DOI: 10.1016/j.resconrec.2016.07.003

[15] ISO 14040. Environmental Management: Life Cycle Assessment: Principles and Framework. Geneva, Switzerland: International Organization for Standardization; 2006

[16] Wu P, Xia B, Zhao X. The importance of use and end-of-life phases to the life cycle greenhouse gas (GHG) emissions of concrete – A review. Renewable and Sustainable Energy Reviews. 2014;**37**:360-369. DOI: 10.1016/j.rser.2014.04.070

[17] Liu K, Leng J. Quantitative research on embodied carbon emissions in the design stage: A case study from an educational building in China. Journal of Asian Architecture and Building Engineering. 2022;**21**(4):1182-1192. DOI: 10.1080/13467581.2022.2046003

[18] Abouhamad M, Abu-Hamd M. Life cycle assessment framework for embodied environmental impacts of building construction systems. Sustainability. 2021;**13**(2):461. DOI: 10.3390/su13020461

[19] Ma M, Li Z, Xue K, Liu M. Exergy-based life cycle assessment model for evaluating the environmental impact of bridge: Principle and case study. Sustainability. 2021;**13**(21):11804. DOI: 10.3390/su132111804

[20] Vitale P, Arena N, Di Gregorio F, Arena U. Life cycle assessment of the end-of-life phase of a residential building. Waste Management. 2017;**60**: 311-321. DOI: 10.1016/j.wasman.2016.10.002

[21] Shi Y, Xu J. BIM-based information system for econo-enviro-friendly end-of-life disposal of construction and demolition waste. Automation in Construction. 2021;**125**:103611. DOI: 10.1016/j.autcon.2021.103611

[22] Haider H, AlMarshod SY, AlSaleem SS, Ali AA, Alinizzi M, Alresheedi M, et al. Life cycle assessment of construction and demolition waste Management in Riyadh, Saudi Arabia. International Journal of Environmental Research and Public Health. 2022;**19**(12): 7382. DOI: 10.3390/ijerph19127382

[23] Wu Z, Shen L, Yu ATW, Zhang X. A comparative analysis of waste management requirements between five green building rating systems for new residential buildings. Journal of Cleaner Production. 2016;**112**:895-902. DOI: 10.1016/j.jclepro.2015.05.073

[24] Nizam RS, Zhang C, Tian L. A BIM based tool for assessing embodied energy for buildings. Energy and Buildings. 2018;**170**:1-14. DOI: 10.1016/j.enbuild.2018.03.067

[25] Wang J, Wei J, Lui Z, Huang C, Du X. Life cycle assessment of building demolition waste based on building information modeling. Resources, Conservation and Recycling. 2022;**178**:

106095. DOI: 10.1016/j.resconrec.2021.106095

[26] Santos R, Aguiar Costa A, Silvestre JD, Pyl L. Development of a BIM-based environmental and economic life cycle assessment tool. Journal of Cleaner Production. 2020;**265**:121705. DOI: 10.1016/j.jclepro.2020.121705

[27] Zimmermann RK, Bruhn S, Birgisdóttir H. BIM-based life cycle assessment of buildings—An investigation of industry practice and needs. Sustainability. 2021;**13**(10):5455. DOI: 10.3390/su13105455

[28] Tecchio P, Gregory J, Ghattas R, Kirchain R. Structured under-specification of life cycle impact assessment data for building assemblies. Journal of Industrial Ecology. 2019;**23**(2):319-334. DOI: 10.1111/jiec.12746

[29] Han B, Leite F. Generic extended reality and integrated development for visualization applications in architecture, engineering, and construction. Automation in Construction. 2022;**140**:104329. DOI: 10.1016/j.autcon.2022.104329

[30] Hu X, Si T, Liu C. Total factor carbon emission performance measurement and development. Journal of Cleaner Production. 2017;**142**:2804-2815. DOI: 10.1016/j.jclepro.2016.10.188

[31] UK Green Building Council. Embodied carbon: developing a client brief. 2017. Available from: https://www.ukgbc.org/wp-content/uploads/2017/09/UK-GBC-EC-Developing-Client-Brief.pdf [Accessed: April 29, 2022]

[32] Cha G-W, Kim Y-C, Moon H, Hong W-H. The effects of data collection method and monitoring of workers' behavior on the generation of demolition waste. International Journal of Environmental Research and Public Health. 2017;**14**(10):1216. DOI: 10.3390/ijerph14101216

[33] Ge J, Luo X, Lu J. Evaluation system and case study for carbon emission of villages in Yangtze River Delta region of China. Journal of Cleaner Production. 2017;**153**:220-229. DOI: 10.1016/j.jclepro.2017.03.144

[34] RICS. Whole life carbon assessment for the built environment. 2017. Available from: https://www.rics.org/globalassets/rics-website/media/upholding-professional-standards/sector-standards/building-surveying/whole-life-carbon-assessment-for-the-built-environment-1st-edition-rics.pdf [Accessed: June 9, 2022]

[35] Gibbon OP, Orr J. How to calculate embodied carbon. Institution of Structural Engineers. 2020. Available from: http://www.https://www.istructe.org/IStructE/media/Public/Resources/istructe-how-to-calculate-embodied-carbon.pdf [Accessed: March 24, 2022]

[36] Department for Business, Energy & Industrial Strategy (BEIS). Greenhouse gas reporting: conversion factors 2021, GOV.UK. 2021. Available from: https://www.gov.uk/government/publications/greenhouse-gas-reporting-conversion-factors-2021 [Accessed: January 18, 2022]

[37] Suh S, d Huppes G. Methods for life cycle inventory of a product. Journal of Cleaner Production. 2005;**13**(7):687-697. DOI: 10.1016/j.jclepro.2003.04.001

[38] Zhu W, Feng W, Li X, Zhang Z. Analysis of the embodied carbon dioxide in the building sector: A case of China. Journal of Cleaner Production. 2020;**269**:

122438. DOI: 10.1016/j.jclepro.2020.
122438

[39] Luo Z, Cang Y, Zhang N, Yang L, Liu J. A quantitative process-based inventory study on material embodied carbon emissions of residential, office, and commercial buildings in China. Journal of Thermal Science. 2019;**28**(6): 1236-1251. DOI: 10.1007/s11630-019-1165-x

[40] Zhang Y, Yan D, Hu S, Guo S. Modelling of energy consumption and carbon emission from the building construction sector in China, a process-based LCA approach. Energy Policy. 2019;**134**:110949. DOI: 10.1016/j.enpol.2019.110949

[41] Coelho A, de Brito J. Environmental analysis of a construction and demolition waste recycling plant in Portugal – Part I: Energy consumption and CO2 emissions. Waste Management. 2013;**33**(5): 1258-1267. DOI: 10.1016/j.wasman.2013.01.025

[42] Coelho A, de Brito J. Environmental analysis of a construction and demolition waste recycling plant in Portugal – Part II: Environmental sensitivity analysis. Waste Management. 2013;**33**(1):147-161. DOI: 10.1016/j.wasman.2012.09.004

[43] Blengini GA. Life cycle of buildings, demolition and recycling potential: A case study in Turin. Italy. Building and Environment. 2009;**44**(2):319-330. DOI: 10.1016/j.buildenv.2008.03.007

Chapter 3

Including Nature-Based Success Measurement Criteria in the Life Cycle Assessment

Miguel Chen Austin and Kimberly Beermann

Abstract

Conventional life cycle assessment (LCA) is a technique to assess environmental impacts associated with all the stages of a product's life or process. Such impacts along the product life or process are assessed via criteria to establish success when accounting for resource intake, waste, and emissions fluxes. In most cases, the assessment range may vary, defined by the designer's and product's aims, failing to evaluate all parts of the said cycle completely. This before is said to follow the "reducing unsustainability" paradigm (RUP), and changes are needed toward an assessment based on the "achieving sustainability" paradigm (ASP). Thus, this chapter embarks on the search for assessment approaches, assuming biomimicry principles can improve current LCIA tools. Comprehending the LCA criteria to assess product or process impacts is done via a literature review. Results showed that most assessment tools continue to be developed under the RUP, where three approaches present great potential for an ASP. A discussion over the difference in assessing two case studies in the built environment, net-zero-energy buildings, and sustainable construction projects under both paradigms is presented.

Keywords: biomimicry, biomimetics, built environment, impact assessment, life cycle assessment, LCA, LCIA, sustainability

1. Introduction

The life cycle assessment (LCA) method aims to assess the product or process's environmental impact along its life cycle [1–3]. This technique or tool focuses mainly on evaluating the contributions that the use of a product or execution of a process has to the overall environmental load. This evaluation may be of help for improvements of the product or process [1]. However, it has been highlighted that LCA works under the premise of "reducing unsustainability" using common indicators to achieve a so-called "eco-design" [4].

Among the four stages found in the ISO14040 guidelines, the LCA starts defining how much of the product life cycle will be evaluated along with the specific purpose of the evaluation. This stage is followed by resources' flux balances, that is, material flux, energy flux, of the product or process and its interaction with the environment, for example, emissions and raw materials consumption. From such resources' flux balances, an inventory analysis is conducted by following a set of indicators belonging to or distributed among various categories. The latter is arranged hierarchically with respect to the impact importance using weighting. The LCA finishes with a critical review of results and results presentation [1, 5].

Measuring a product's life cycle to reduce unsustainability intends to reduce its environmental impacts, but this may not help create sustainability [4] of the product or process because their continuity is yet to be considered, along with the conditions that assure the need for that product or process. In turn, the product or process assessment toward improvement needs to be based on achieving sustainability rather than reducing the negative impacts on the environment [4].

Assessment measures toward improvement based on achieving sustainability have been argued to be needed, where the design approaches, cradle-to-cradle, and biomimicry, are the closest aligned with sustainability achievement, aiming at creating beneficial impacts [4].

Thus, accounting for the previously presented arguments, does the conventional LCA method need a revision to change the paradigm? (i.e., achieving sustainability, **Figure 1**). Could the biomimicry philosophy help improve the current LCA method?

These two questions have led to a comprehensive yet systematic review based on a combination of keywords framed in the specific topic. Thus, the first keyword combination is Biomimicry AND ("life cycle assessment" OR LCA) on the Google Scholar database, without year restrictions. This keyword combination search yielded 2600 results. The same search in the ScienceDirect database yielded 216 results, among

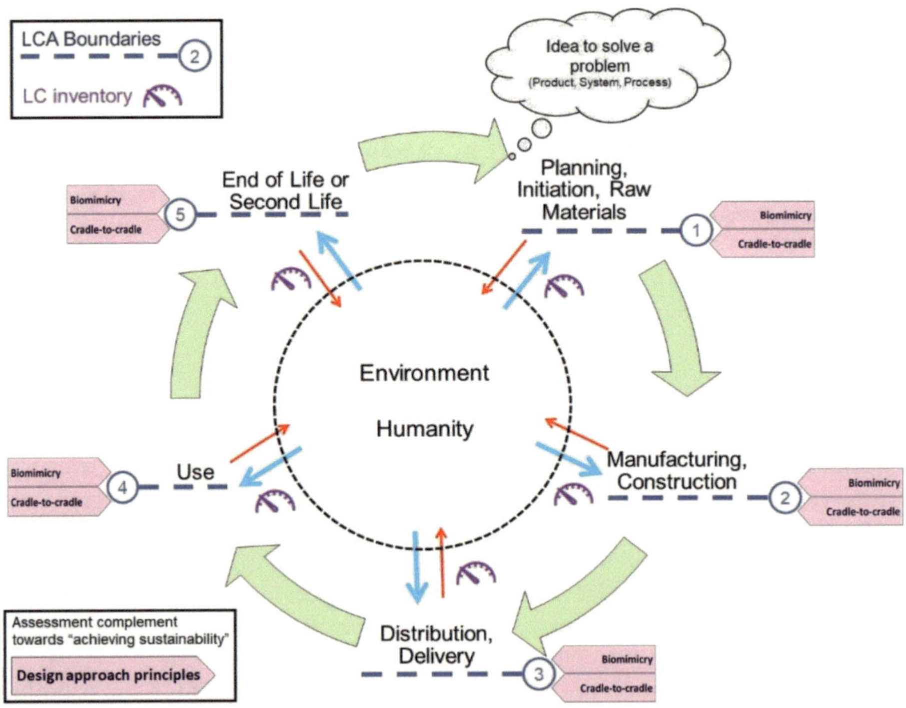

Figure 1.
Representation of a life cycle highlighting the inventory fluxes (inputs in blue, outputs in red) and impact assessment stages. Biomimicry principles (in pink) could act as an assessment complement toward developing a tool that evaluates sustainability achievement.

which 34 results were irrelevant documents such as part of books, for example, index and foreword.

This systematic literature search was analyzed using the VOSviewer software [6] to examine current research trends. Based on 210 documents, network, and overlay visualization maps are constructed using a compiled .ris file with the metadata of each document. Such maps can be created by using two approaches key terms in the keywords section from each research article or key terms in the title and abstract of each document, both based on a minimum threshold of occurrence of the key terms. The following observations can be drawn from the maps presented in **Figures 2–4**.

When using the recommended minimum threshold by the software algorithm, based on the occurrence of the keywords, the overlay visualization (**Figure 2**) presents the term "biomimicry." This term does not disappear for any minimum threshold in the keywords' occurrence approach. The contrary happens when the terms in the title and abstract are employed until the threshold is lower than six.

Nevertheless, in both approaches, the term "biomimicry" appeared as a topic of losing interest, that is, this term is not included as part of the titles, abstracts, and keywords in documents after 2016. That was seven years ago. The same appeared to happen with the term "biomimetics." This is worth mentioning because the interchangeability of both terms is still mistakenly employed among researchers, architects, and designers using nature as a source of inspiration. A clear and straightforward analysis of similarities and differences can be found in [7, 8].

Conversely to the no-use of the terms "biomimicry" and "biomimetics," the prefix "bio" is frequently spotted in recent documents (color yellow), which actually is intended to be referred to the same perspective as "inspired by nature." This indicates that cautiousness is still prompted to use the most meaningful terms when asking to what extent you are letting the design be inspired by nature: "biomimicry" or "biomimetics." Attention should be paid to this issue since a design solution "biologically inspired" does not intrinsically imply that the design solution is "nature-based" (**Figure 5**) because the former is embedded within the definitions of nature-based

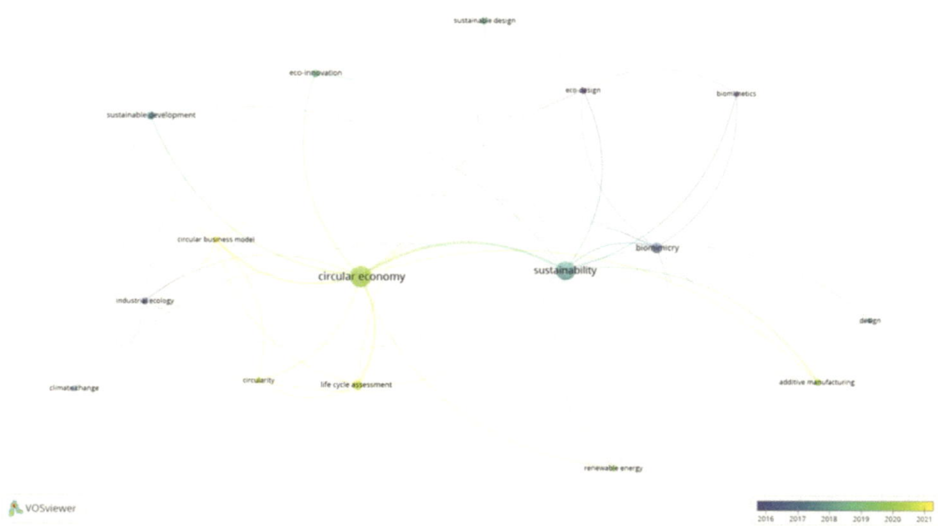

Figure 2.
Overlay representation of the keyword occurrence approach, using the minimum occurrence threshold (16).

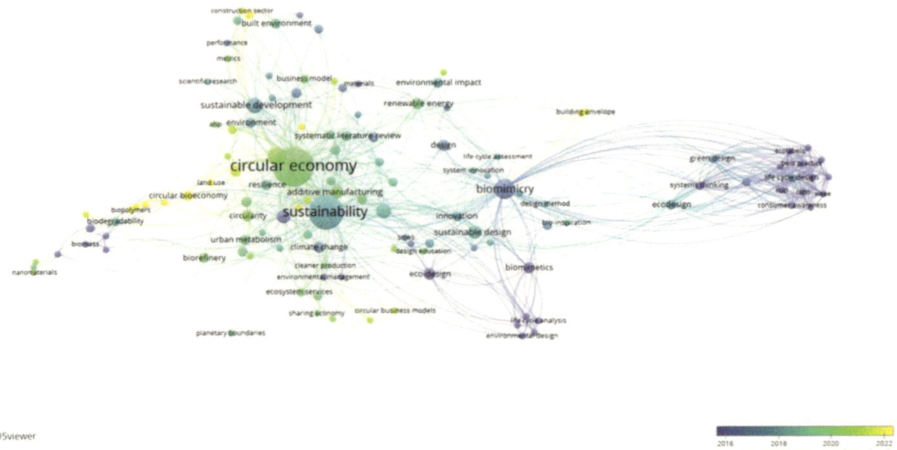

Figure 3.
Overlay representation of the keyword occurrence approach, using an occurrence threshold of two.

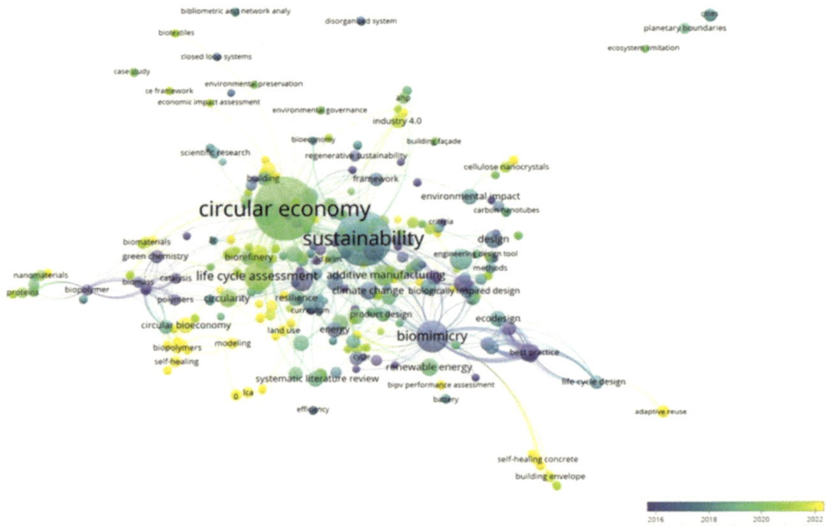

Figure 4.
Overlay representation of the keyword occurrence approach, using an occurrence threshold of one.

solutions [9]. In addition, the use of the term "biomimetic system" was recently coined by the International Standard Organization (ISO) 18,458:2015 (recently reviewed and confirmed in 2021) [10], which claims: "... If a technical system is subjected to a development process according to this International Standard, then it is allowed to be referred to as a 'biomimetic' system" [10].

Moreover, specifically to the keyword occurrence approach (**Figures 2–4**), three terms appeared as having higher relevance in descending order: "circular economy," "sustainability," and "biomimicry." This tendency is also presented regarding timeline interests (**Figures 2–4**). On the other hand, the keyword "LCA" or "life cycle assessment" is not as frequently spotted as expected for a literature search based primarily on these keywords. Although this is before, it is interesting to observe how closely these two keywords are to the keyword "circular economy" based on a timeline

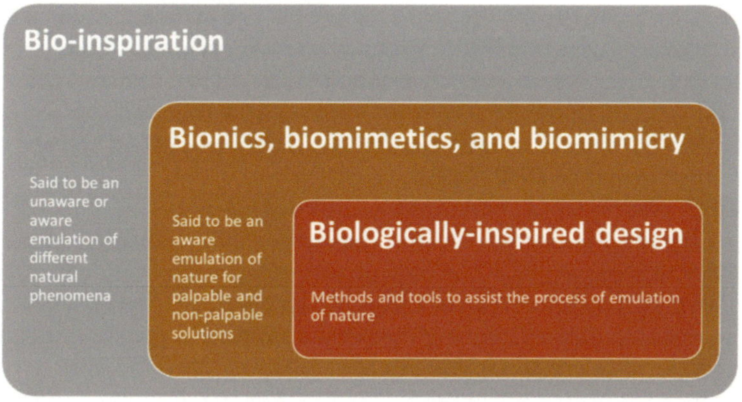

Figure 5.
Proposal for providing understanding and connections among the terms involved in the methods and processes using biological analogies (adapted from [9]).

interest (**Figures 2–4**, in yellow). This shows the elevated attention paid to economic aspects, which is highlighted by other keywords in recent documents (in yellow): "circularity," "circular bioeconomy," "circular business model," "business model," "construction sector" (one of the most important contributors to the global economy), and "land use," and "... material." Regardless, the most frequent keywords "circular economy" and "sustainability" (**Figures 2–4**) are part of the objectives for which a designer carries out a LCA whether the scope of the assessment is the environmental, social, or economic impact of the product or process throughout its life cycle.

2. LCA as known today

This section first introduces the theoretical knowledge about the life cycle assessment methods and finishes with the measurement criteria. The LCA method can help designers to account for and analyze the environmental impact caused by the product or process on the environment throughout their entire life cycle. This analysis includes the effect of the inputs required (i.e., resources) and consequent outputs (e.g., emissions) of such products or processes [2].

Considering that the CLCA method has a flexible component that allows the designer to concentrate on evaluating the product or process for a specific purpose, three levels of assessment can be encountered in the literature [11]: conceptual, simplified, and detailed. The following subsections give more details about such levels, phases, and variants found in the literature.

2.1 LCA variants

Since the first implications of setting up a method to evaluate the environmental impacts of a product or process in the 1960s, many improvements have been intertwined with its original concept definition, looking to continue to take advantage of its benefits. Nevertheless, limitations have been presented since the first implementation of the LCA, for example, listed in [12]. Two of those limitations concern the research questions of this chapter: weighting and other aspects of sustainability (economic and social). In this matter, many variants of the LCA can be found in the literature, which copes with the two limitations. For instance, studies focusing efforts on combining these two limitations are: the life cycle sustainability assessment (LCSA) [13], life cycle impact assessment (LCIA) [14], and an LCA + C2C but accounts for the three pillars of sustainability [15]. Other variants are economic life-cycle costing [3], the social LCA (SLCA) [16], dynamic LCA [17], and positive sustainability performance (PSP) [13].

Moreover, attributional LCA (ALCA) and consequential LCA (CLCA) [18] are said to be two approaches to the LCA [5]. The former relates strongly to the evaluation of a system's specific impact or optimization potential, recommended for micro-level (or local scale) [18]. The latter relates to the impact that a change on a system could have or the increase in demand for such system's function or product, recommended for meso/macro level (or regional/global scale) [18].

Specifically, in the built environment, the ALCA is the dominant system boundary selected, following the EN15804 (or EN15978) [19], shaping most policy decisions on buildings regarding environmental and climate aspects [18].

2.2 LCA phases and impact assessment criteria

The effect of the inputs and output on the environment can be quantified by the LCA method in different ways because it may vary with the field of application, the first phase of its methodology being the establishment of the objective and scope [20]. However, all products and processes may share the same inputs and outputs. For the former, the inputs are raw materials, water, energy, and chemical resources [2]. For the latter, the outputs are products, co-products, solid waste, and emissions in the air, water, and soil [2]. Detailing every aspect of these inputs and outputs is referred to as the life cycle inventory (LCI) inventory analysis, where they are quantified throughout their life cycle after their identification. Specifically, compiling an LCI starts with process analysis, or a bottom-up approach, where the product system analyzed is broken down into a series of processes representing the life cycle of a product. This is followed by an environmentally extended input-output analysis or a top-down approach rooted in macroeconomics. Finally, a hybrid analysis involves combining the previous two approaches. Each approach requires modeling a system using specific production processes or entire economic systems [21].

The effect of such input harvesting and outputs on the environment are normally measured at different scales: local, regional, and global [2], but also through various forms. This part represents the life cycle impact assessment [22] and is based on the results of the LCI [20]. Among these forms of effect quantification or measurement are cradle-to-grave [ref], cradle-to-gate [ref], gate-to-gate, and the cradle-to-cradle [ref], also referred to as main boundaries for LCA [12] (the limits in which the analysis is performed).

For these different scales of effects, the LCA is known to measure them [2, 23] by using footprint measurements, for example, carbon [24], water [25] (ecological footprint [26] when combined with carbon), and energy. Besides, acidification [27], eutrophication [28], ozone depletion potential [29], photochemical oxidation potential [30], smog, depletion of biotic and abiotic resources, land use, and damages such as ecotoxicity [31], and human toxicity.

In literature, these effects are categorized by the approach used to describe the environmental mechanism of impact depending on the LCI output [23]: midpoint (problem-oriented or classical) and endpoint (damage-oriented) approaches. The former concerns phenomenon-based environmental issues [32], while the latter concerns environmental impacts leading to damage [23]. The main difference between these two approaches is based on the level of uncertainty associated with indicators' calculation regarding the environmental mechanism related to the environmental issue (for the midpoint approach), and to the prompting of the damage, in context (in the endpoint approach) to human health, ecosystems, and resources availability [33].

All these measurement criteria in the LCA method, specifically in the impact assessment phase, can also be assessed via software such as SimaPro [34], GaBi [35], Umberto [36], One Click LCA [37], and OpenLCA [38].

For impact assessment in the life cycle, several methods can be found in the literature (an overview of each is provided in [23]): Eco-indicator'99, CML 2001, EDIP 2003, EPS 2000, EPD 2007, Ecological Scarcity 2006, Impact 2002+, Recipe, TRACI, Ecological Scarcity Method, Single indicator methods such as ecological and carbon footprints, ILCD 2011, and USEtox.

As the last step of the LCA methodology, there is the interpretation of the scope and objective, inventory, and impact analysis, in order to recognize and address environmental, health, and resource consumption pressures [39].

Moreover, the cradle-to-cradle life cycle approach is aligned with circular economy objectives. For a building, it is the process of carrying out the construction and the building itself [40]. Briefly, this would be divided into four phases [41, 42]: product, construction, use, and end of life, but a more detailed approach it can be given in the product and use phase [40].

Defining the process and factors, it would be as follows:

- Product: related to the initiation and design for construction [40], it considers the materials and their supply, the manufacturing behind, and the management services, where transportation is included [41, 42]. Its main quantitative factors are the coal included in extraction, manufacture, diligence, and disposal of materials, the inputs in relation to energy and water, and the waste outputs [43].

- Construction: execution of construction (transport, construction itself, and installation) [41] and implementation of the necessary measures to mitigate negative impacts [40]. At this stage, the inputs are water and energy, which generally has a significant waste impact [43].

- Use: is the focus of impact and conditions of use [42], where the findings of its maintenance will consequently involve replacement and refurbishment actions [41].

- End of life: refers to cases where the building has demolition as well as the ease of reuse and recycling [42, 43]. All outputs of the process are considered for utilization and quantified in a process called benefits and burdens beyond the system boundary [42].

Although a design phase is not included in the literature in terms of inputs and outputs, it has been placed by the relevance of the planning strategy, concept, and technical design [42]. It allows maximizing results, evaluation of costs, benefits, and combination of designs [40], providing greater inclusion of practices in the process, advancing more toward efficiency than only mitigating impacts. This is why beyond including a social and economic life cycle [44], to complement a focus on sustainable totality, the limits of improvement toward efficiency, innovation, decision, and compliance with circular economy must be addressed, where the inspiration in nature can provide opportunities. Hence the following section shows an analysis of the literature using nature as inspiration for the specific chapter topic.

3. Nature moto as a source of inspiration

Forms, behaviors, and processes in nature have been a source of inspiration for many innovative approaches for products, systems, and process designs, for example, bionics, biomimetics, and biomimicry, in different stages of corporate sustainability (compliance and business-centered, systemic, and regenerative and co-evolutionary, respectively) and worldview (technocentric, mixed, and eco-centric, respectively) [7]. The approach cradle-to-cradle is a regenerative design approach based on biomimicry principles, that is, use materials sparingly, use energy efficiently, do not exhaust resources, sources or buy locally, optimize the whole rather than maximize each component individually, do not pollute your nest, remain in dynamic equilibrium with the biosphere, using waste as a resource, diversify and cooperate, and be informed and share information [45].

3.1 Improving impact assessment

Almost a decade ago, it was argued that no impact assessment method had been developed for biomimicry and that current ways of impact assessment followed a "reduced unsustainability" paradigm instead of following an "achieving sustainability" paradigm [4]. This "achieving sustainability" paradigm is not entirely opposed to the conventional way of performing impact assessment. However, these paradigms differ from each other as follows [4]:

1. While the conventional paradigm considers all potentially harmful impacts, the new paradigm considers all impacts in context.

2. Instead of comparing the product characteristics with other products, it is proposed to assess the product against sustainability conditions. Such assessment needs designers to distinguish between "what is" and "what is not" sustainable. For example, if a product has a characteristic that is beneficial to various aspects of the indoor environment but is not to one aspect of human life, the product would not be considered as having a beneficial impact.

3. Contrary to assessing progress, it is proposed to evaluate "achievement" in the sense of whether the target design characteristics are met. In this way, for instance, instead of focusing on developing systems, products, or processes to help reduce energy consumption from fossil fuels, the target is considered to function with an alternative energy source.

Having a beneficial impact, here, refers to the impact on the environment contributing to the regeneration of that environment toward a sustainable state [4]. Internalizing such a new paradigm helps enlighten how the impacts are assessed, highlighting the product benefits to sustainability's environmental, social, and economic aspects.

Recent studies found in the literature present potential to materialize such a new-paradigm-based tool based on biomimetics [46], on biomimicry [40], and on cradle-to-cradle (C2C, also known as regenerative design approach) [15]. These studies followed the ten biomimicry principles [45]. **Table 1** presents a comparison of these three approaches.

Moreover, Terrier et al. [46], in 2019, proposed an assistance tool to provide a quantitative performance tool for biomimetic-based designs. This tool has been developed as a complement to the ISO 1845 standard. In this tool, the ten principles of biomimicry are grouped into three dimensions of biomimetics design: Efficiency and frugality, preservation and resilience, and circularity and systemic approach. Whether this tool is based on biomimicry or biomimetics, or the authors used these terms to refer to the same, needs to be clarified. However, this tool only assesses the environmental impact of the biomimetic design based on the midpoint approach in the LCIA, not including quantifications for other aspects of sustainability, that is, economy and society. Such a tool for impact assessment of biomimetic design still follows the "reduced unsustainability" paradigm due to the questions and metrics employed [46].

Furthermore, Peralta et al. [15], in 2021, proposed an upgrade to the cradle-to-cradle approach (a form of biomimicry) for sustainable designs. Since for the cradle-to-cradle approach there are not yet reported normative and guidelines, considering only environmental and social aspects qualitatively without any available tool, the proposed upgrade intends to assess both positive and negative impacts by dividing the assessment into three levels, that is, evaluating the LCI at micro, meso, and macro levels. At the micro level, the calculations are based on midpoint indicators; thus, they do not account for the entire context. At the meso level, the quality of the resources (or inputs) is evaluated. Finally, at the macro level, future effects are considered, including calculations for optimal design, allowing more sustainable product versions. The latter indicates that this proposed upgrade (or methodology) finalizes with assessing the product's progress, which coincides with the "reduction of unsustainability" paradigm. Despite this, this proposed methodology advances the field by providing a quantitative tool for complementing the cradle-to-cradle approach [15].

Finally, later in the same year, among the interest in considering sustainability, a different approach based on biomimicry may have potential application toward the "achieving sustainability" paradigm. This approach, referred to as the "Biocircular model" by Beermann and Austin [40], is a conceptual nature-inspired approach built upon the sustainability consideration discrepancies among sustainable construction projects. Following the problem-based approach [47, 48], this Biocircular model is founded upon various biomimicry principles, combined with the circular economy and sustainability, leading to four supporting qualitative valuations, that is, active (A), behavior (B), housing (H), and share (S), that helps include sustainability as a target to the problem considered. Here, a complete qualitative analysis is presented for the six phases of construction projects, ending with the delivery phase, which was then supported by surveying experts in the field. Thus, as a qualitative approach that looks for the sustainability target in each phase of the construction projects individually, it coincides with the new paradigm previously mentioned. However, no quantitative criteria are provided [40]. Besides, existing indicators were contrasted with the Biocircular model approach, and none fulfilled the four supporting valuations. In contrast, four existing qualitative indicators did fulfill the supporting valuations: Reuse of construction elements [49], reuse of excavation materials for backfill [49], use of local material to reduce emissions [49], and water reuse system [50]. In a sense, this also follows the cradle-to-cradle principles.

Achieving sustainability paradigm [4]			LCA	Potential impact assessment tools		
Constituents		**Description**	Conventional and current variants	BiomiMETRIC, 2019 [46]	LCA + C2C, 2021 [15]	Biocircular model, 2021 [40]
Life cycle approach		Analyzing each step in the life of a product, from its conception to its end.				
"Consider all impacts in context"		By including context, the impacts occurring in the product life cycle are evaluated as beneficial or potentially harmful.				
"Assess to conditions of sustainability"	Environment	Comparing analysis with existing products' solution is no longer required. The product is sustainable in its life cycle, or it is not.		*	*	**
	Social				**	**
	Economic				**	**
"Assess achievement"		A sustainable solution is assessed by achieving, rather than by reflecting progress improvement of existing solutions toward sustainability.				

The color indicates potentially promising. *Provide a detailed way for calculation (quantitative).* **Qualitative.*

Table 1.
Evaluation of recent potential nature-inspired tools for impact assessment toward sustainability against the "achieving sustainability" paradigm.

3.2 Biomimicry, circularity, and sustainability in buildings

Now, a brief look into the applications of the arguments previously presented from the point of view of the built environment, specifically to sustainable construction projects such as net-zero-energy (NZE) buildings or green buildings.

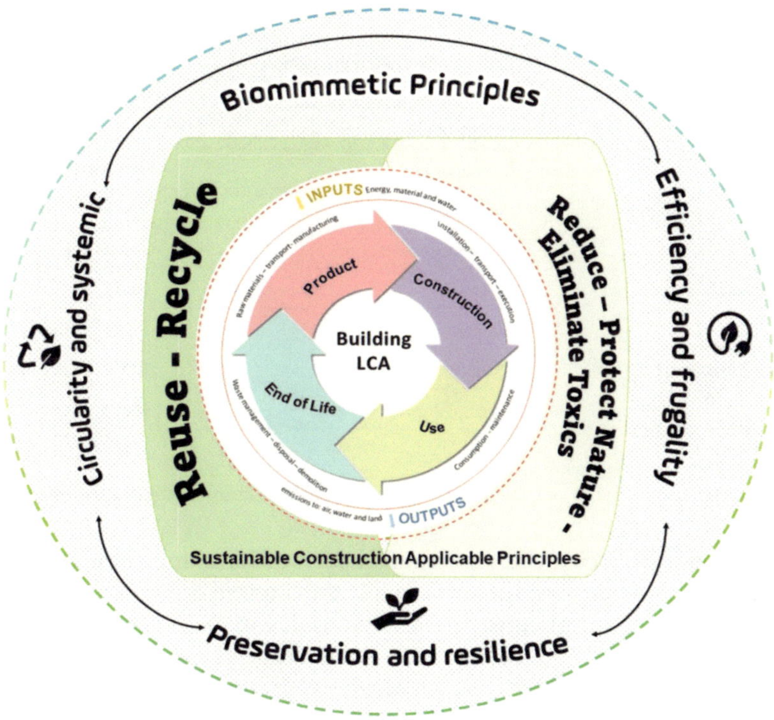

Figure 6.
Principles of sustainable buildings and biomimetic design applicable to the life cycle of a building.

Although the BiomiMETRIC tool [46] has an environmental dimension, in conjunction with the principles of sustainable construction [41], principles applicable to the LCA stages of a building were identified and can be visualized in **Figure 6**. While it is true that achieving sustainability requires going beyond the environmental impact, it is notorious that LCA can maximize its scope and approach, where the use of a second life through circularity in materials and components can have great benefits [39]. In the principles for biomimetic design, circularity is complemented by systematization, and beyond environmental preservation, resilience is addressed [46], which is a more developed degree of adaptation.

Another approach not included in the sustainable principles but found in the Green Building Rating Systems (GBRT) [42] is efficiency and optimization, one of the most highlighted points when applying a biomimetic methodology to solve a problem. It should be emphasized that another challenge within the principles and their application is to maintain consistency between the different phases. In GBRT, the environmental dimension predominates with the number of indicators, while the construction and end-of-life phases have the fewest indicators [42].

In **Table 2**, matching principles were identified between [46] and [41] in order to obtain pinnacles, that is, biological entities that attend or act according to the established principles, applying the biomimetic methodology of "Living envelope" [51] complemented by the AskNature tool [52] from the Biomimicry Institute.

Based on the pinnacles found by [40], the inspirational capabilities in nature are illustrated:

Area	Principle	Pinnacles
Efficiency and frugality	Reduce resource consumption	Bees
	Efficiency of materials and water/energy consumption	Eastern oyster/plants
	Source or buy local	Sacworm
Preservation and resilience	Protect nature	Earthworm
	Eliminate toxics	American Beaver
Circularity and Systemic approach	Reuse	Birds
	Recycle	Protoplasm of a protozoan
Design and Management	Quality	Bird (zebra finch)
	Diversify and cooperate	Meerkats

Table 2.
Pinnacles identified that meet the principles of biomimetics and sustainable construction according to area.

- In the case of efficiency, there are several options for inspiration, such as bees, who forge their hives with the principle of storing the greatest amount of honey with the least amount of construction material, wax. While the oriental oyster already has a case of biomimicry by creating a type of calcium carbonate cement with softer and stickier features, which allows greater resistance to tides. In the use of the local, the sack worm utilizes materials around it, such as twigs and leaves, to build protection boxes.

- In environmental protection, beavers are examples of ecosystem engineers that shape entire landscapes, and earthworms add air and nutrients to the soil. By consuming organic matter, they decompose it to make it less harmful and excrete nutrients. Others, such as a protozoan, which feeds and creates its building elements, and birds, who always use materials at their disposal, including decomposed wood for their nests. This process for birds is essential, as they are also an example of quality because of the relevance and complexity of their construction, materials, and speed since their ability to reproduce depends on it.

In addition to the principles mentioned in **Figure 6**, design and management principles, such as quality and cooperation, were added in **Table 2** to broaden the areas of principles that do not apply to the life cycle itself but are present in its formulation, strategy, and control, and which are increasingly becoming a necessity in early design [53]. Other principles regarding decentralization, such as diversity, redundancy, and independence, were not considered, as they can be included at the qualitative level of planning and management [54].

4. Discussion

The discussion of this chapter must start by framing the research questions presented at the beginning. Does the conventional LCA method need revision to change the paradigm? (i.e., achieving sustainability). The LCA method has been a research topic dating back to around 1997. As presented in previous sections, many variants and improvements to the LCA four phases can be found. Thus, rather than a revision

Design alternatives	Aspects to assess during usage phase	Sustainability aspects	Constituents for assessing the design alternatives	
			Assessing progress (as compared with existing no NZEB buildings)	**Assessing achievement (under the "if it would be" and binary orientation of sustainability [55])**
New NZE building*	Electricity consumption	Environmental	80% of electricity consumption reduction as compared with existing no NZEB buildings.	Electricity consumption constraints are met to the limit they can be supplied by renewable sources.
	Electricity generation		20% of electricity generation comes from renewable sources.	Energy autonomy is achieved. Function 100% on renewable energy generated on site.
	Thermal comfort and IAQ	Social welfare	Thermal discomfort is reduced and IAQ is improved.	100% of occupants' indoor safety air quality is achieved.
	Costs**	Economical	Resources used can be provided by markets. Predictive maintenance	Predictive maintenance is automated. Systems lives are longer.
Retrofitted NZE building*	Electricity consumption	Environmental	70–90% of electricity consumption reduction via improvements in HVAC systems and envelope.	100% of electricity consumption are supplied by renewable sources.
	Electricity generation		10–30% of electricity generated comes from renewable sources on site	Energy autonomy is achieved. Function 100% on renewable energy generated on site.
	Thermal comfort and IAQ	Social welfare	90% harmful pathogens reduction.	Pathogens levels are continuously monitored to avoid risks.
	Costs**	Economical	A 10% reduction of resources used from other no-local markets. Maintenance (corrective and predictive) plans are improved.	Resources used are only provided by markets. Systems lives are longer.

**Systems with normal levels of automation.*
***Costs are related to resources and maintenance.*

Table 3.
Differences in the assessment outcomes of two building design alternatives when using different constituents for the assessment (using [4] as reference for other case studies).

of the entire method is well-established, a broadening of its LCIA boundaries [4] and interpretation phase is needed. The former helps the designers to think beyond the "this product solves this specific problem and is better than the others" toward "this product is beneficial because it solves this specific problem, and no collateral impact is created at present nor in future scenarios." Here, the context is crucial [4], and thus, instead of letting the designer choose the impact assessment boundaries through its life cycle, it could reflect an advancement to the current variants of LCA.

However, encountered impact assessment tools still struggle to assess the achievement of sustainability of the product but assure advancement in the LCIA current indicators. Although the other two tools [15, 46] provide a quantitative framework for the LCIA, the Biocircular model [40] does not solely focus on providing a way of measuring sustainability but rather on working as a complement to the problem analyzed. This potential could be convenient to how LCIA is performed and interpreted in years to come, but the approach is in its early stages.

Hence, this brings us to our next research question. Could the biomimicry philosophy help improve the current LCA method? By highlighting the fundamentals and potential of the approaches encountered (Section 3), all three are based on biomimicry principles, including the cradle-to-cradle approach, which has its basis in a regenerative stage [7].

To demonstrate the application of the achieving sustainability assessment paradigm to the built environment, for instance, consider a net zero energy (NZE) design target for a new building and an existing building retrofitted toward the net zero target. **Table 3** provides an approach to assess both building designs following the current LCA and the new paradigm. This is done only for the usage phase among the building life cycle but considers all three aspects of sustainability.

Other examples can be also assessed, for instance, positive energy buildings. In this case, the surplus is exported to provide and share with nearby buildings. Another

Design	**Aspects to assess during usage phase**	**Sustainability aspects**	**Constituents for assessing the design alternatives**	
			Assessing progress (as compared with existing no sustainable construction projects)	**Assessing achievement (under the "if it would be" and binary orientation of sustainability** [55]**)**
Sustainable construction project	Waste production	Environmental	20% waste production reduced.	Construction waste was recycled and reused in other projects as a resource.
	Life quality	Social welfare	The life-lost rate is reduced to 1%.	No lives lost.
	Economic contribution	Economical	The unemployment rate was reduced by 10%.	The employment rate increased by 10%.

Table 4.
Differences in the assessment outcomes of a sustainable construction design project when using different constituents for the assessment (taking [40] as reference).

example is sustainable construction projects. **Table 4** presents an example of the binary orientation applied to the sustainable construction project under the "achieving sustainability" paradigm, taking as a reference the work of [40].

Moreover, a significant amount of quantitative and qualitative impact assessment indicators for sustainable construction projects are found in the literature. Such indicators can also be applicable to the impact assessment of other products or processes. However, it was noticed by [40] that none of the quantitative indicators have any limitations or threshold to offer a limit value that needs to be reached or passed in order to be considered as sustainable. Thinking about such limit value falls into the relative orientation of sustainability proposed by [55].

5. Conclusions

This chapter reviews the life cycle assessment method, its stages, and methods for impact assessment. Many LCA variants have been proposed to include other aspects of sustainability, that is, social (SLCA) and economic (life cycle costs), rather than only accounting for environmental impacts. Although many improvements have been proposed to the original LCA method version, the flexibility associated with framing the LCA boundaries according to the designer's willingness stands out to assess the product's impacts over its life cycle. This flexibility makes it difficult to push new design paradigms to achieve true sustainability in context. The biomimetic design approach follows such a design paradigm since it looks for natural inspiration but limits its focus to solving human problems.

On the other hand, biomimicry design approaches go further toward strictly achieving sustainability under the binary orientation. This before led us to ask whether biomimicry can help improve the current LCA method's way of evaluating impacts, following the "nature success" philosophy. The literature analysis suggests that most impact assessment tools today still struggle to evaluate from the point of view of "achieving sustainability" instead of "reducing unsustainability." Among the tools found, three potential tools based on biomimicry principles are analyzed. Only two provide detailed quantitative criteria but only for the environmental aspect and following the constituents of "assess to conditions of sustainability." However, although these two tools greatly advance the current frameworks to evaluate impacts for biomimetic-based and cradle-to-cradle-based designs, they still present limitations on "assessing achievement" since their criteria reflects the assessment of progress improvement. Conversely, the Biocircular model approach offers great potential to frame the "achieving sustainability" paradigm since it still is in the early stages of development.

Moreover, two case studies were analyzed under the constituents of "achieving sustainability" and "assessing progress": (i) a net zero energy building by comparing a new design with a design to retrofit, and (ii) a sustainable construction project. Both cases are analyzed under the usage phase of the life cycle.

Finally, the present work, by presenting the analysis of current LCIA tools from the point of view of the "achieving sustainability" paradigm, hopes to bring the attention of designers and engineers, especially to the construction sector. Urgency is required due to a rapid shortage of resources and a deliberate (or unintentional) increase in waste production.

Acknowledgements

The authors would like to thank the Technological University of Panama and the Faculty of Mechanical Engineering (https://fim.utp.ac.pa/, accessed on 18 January 2023) for their collaboration, together with the Research Group ECEB (https://eceb.utp.ac.pa/, accessed on 18 January 2023). The authors would also like to acknowledge the Chevening Scholarship program along the Geography Department at Birkbeck, University of London. This research was funded by a Panamanian Institution Secretaría Nacional de Ciencia, Tecnología e Innovación (SENACYT) https://www.senacyt.gob.pa/ (accessed on 18 January 2023), together with the Sistema Nacional de Investigación (SNI) SNI30-2021.

Conflict of interest

The authors declare no conflict of interest.

Author details

Miguel Chen Austin[1*] and Kimberly Beermann[2,3]

1 Faculty of Mechanical Engineering, Technological University of Panama, Panama City, Panama

2 Geography Department, Birkbeck, University of London, London, UK

3 Technological University of Panama, Panama City, Panama

*Address all correspondence to: miguel.chen@utp.ac.pa

References

[1] Muralikrishna IV, Manickam V. Life Cycle Assessment. In: Environmental Management. India: Butterworth-Heinemann, Elsevier; 2017. pp. 57-75. ISBN: 978-0-12-811989-1

[2] Muthu SS. Ways of measuring the environmental impact of textile processing: An overview. In: Assessing the Environmental Impact of Textiles and the Clothing Supply Chain. United Kingdom: Woodhead Publishing Elsevier; 2020. pp. 33-56. eISBN: 978-1-78242-112-2

[3] Di Maria A, Eyckmans J, Van Acker K. Use of LCA and LCC to help decision-making between downcycling versus recycling of construction and demolition waste. In: Advances in Construction and Demolition Waste Recycling. India: Woodhead Publishing, Elsevier; 2020. pp. 537-558. eISBN: 978-0-12-819056-2

[4] de Pauw IC, Kandachar P, Karana E. Assessing sustainability in nature-inspired design. International Journal of Sustainable Engineering. 2015;**8**(1):5-13

[5] European Commission, Joint Research Centre, institute for environment sustainability. In: International Reference Life Cycle Data System (ILCD): Handbook -General Guide for Life Cycle Assessment - Detailed Guidance [Internet]. First Edit. Luxembourg: Publications Office of the European Union; 2010. Available from: https://publications.jrc.ec.europa.eu/repository/handle/111111111/15651

[6] Centre for Science and Technology Studies. VOSviewer - Visualizing Scientific Landscapes. The Netherlands: Leiden University; 2023. Available from: https://www.vosviewer.com/

[7] Landrum NE, Mead T. Sustainability in the Biom*. In: Environmental Footprints and Eco-Design of Products and Processes. Singapore: Springer; 2022. pp. 1-15. Available from: https://link.springer.com/chapter/10.1007/978-981-19-1812-4_1. eISBN: 978-981-19-1812-4

[8] Palombini FL, Muthu SS. Bionics and Sustainable Design. Singapore: Springer; 2022. p. 40

[9] Bianciardi A, Becattini N, Cascini G. How would nature design and implement nature-based solutions? Nature-Based Solutions. 2023;**3**:100047. Available from: https://linkinghub.elsevier.com/retrieve/pii/S2772411522000398

[10] International Organization for Standardization. ISO 18458:2015 - Biomimetics — Terminology, Concepts and Methodology. Geneva Switzerland: International Organization for Standardization; 2021. Available from: https://www.iso.org/standard/62500.html

[11] Farjana SH, Mahmud MAP, Huda N. Introduction to life cycle assessment. In: Life Cycle Assessment for Sustainable Mining. India: Butterworth-Heinemann, Elsevier; 2021. pp. 1-13. ISBN: 978-0-12-811989-1

[12] Torabi F, Ahmadi P. Battery technologies. In: Simulation of Battery Systems. Academic Press, Elsevier; 2020. pp. 1-54. ISBN: 978-0-12-816212-5

[13] Kühnen M, Silva S. From negative to positive sustainability performance measurement and assessment ? A qualitative inquiry drawing on framing effects theory. Business Strategy and the Environment. 2021;**2022**:1985-2001

[14] Cowie AL, Brandão M, Soimakallio S. Quantifying the climate effects of forest-based bioenergy. In: Managing Global

Warming: An Interface of Technology and Human Issues. India: Academic Press, Elsevier; 2019. pp. 399-418. ISBN 978-0-12-814104-5

[15] Peralta ME, Alcalá N, Soltero VM. Weighting with life cycle assessment and cradle to cradle: A methodology for global sustainability design. Applied Sciences. MDPI. 2021;**11**(19):9042

[16] European Environment Agency. Life Cycle Assessment (LCA)—A guide to approaches, experiences and information sources [Internet]. 1998. Available from: https://www.eea.europa.eu/publications/GH-07-97-595-EN-C

[17] Turner C, Oyekan J, Garn W, Duggan C, Abdou K. Industry 5.0 and the circular economy: Utilizing LCA with intelligent products. Sustainability. 2022;**14**(22):14847

[18] Hansen RN, Rasmussen FN, Ryberg M, Birgisdóttir H. A systematic review of consequential LCA on buildings: the perspectives and challenges of applications and inventory modelling. International Journal of Life Cycle Assessment. 2022;**1**:1-15. Available from: https://link.springer.com/article/10.1007/s11367-022-02126-w

[19] Andersen SC, Birgisdottir H, Birkved M. Life cycle assessments of circular economy in the built environment—A scoping review. Sustainability. MDPI. 2022;**14**(11):6887

[20] Kamali M, Hewage K, Sadiq R. Conventional versus modular construction methods: A comparative cradle-to-gate LCA for residential buildings. Energy and Buildings. 2019;**1**(204):109479

[21] Crawford RH, Bontinck PA, Stephan A, Wiedmann T, Yu M. Hybrid life cycle inventory methods – A review. Journal of Cleaner Production. 2018;**20**(172):1273-1288

[22] APC C, Darko A, Ameyaw EE. Strategies for promoting green building technologies adoption in the construction industry—An International Study. Sustainability. 2017;**9**:969. Available from: https://www.mdpi.com/2071-1050/9/6/969/htm

[23] Muthu SS. Estimating the overall environmental impact of textile processing: Life cycle assessment of textile products. In: Assessing the Environmental Impact of Textiles and the Clothing Supply Chain. United Kingdom: Woodhead Publishing, Elsevier; 2020. pp. 105-129. ISBN: 978-1-78242-112-2 (online)

[24] Muthu SS. Carbon footprints. In: Muthu SS, editor. Environmental Footprints and Eco-design of Products and Processes. Singapore: Springer Singapore; 2019. Available from: http://link.springer.com/10.1007/978-981-13-7912-3

[25] Muthu SS. Water footprint. In: Muthu SS, editor. Environmental Footprints and Eco-design of Products and Processes. Singapore: Springer Singapore; 2021. Available from: http://link.springer.com/10.1007/978-981-33-4377-1. eBook ISBN: 978-981-33-4377-1

[26] Wackernagel M, Beyers B. Ecological Footprint - Managing our Biocapacity Budget. Canada: New Society Publishers; 2019. p. 288. ISBN: 9780865719118

[27] Geller W, Schultze M. Acidification. In: Encyclopedia of Inland Waters. Academic Press, Elsevier; 2009. pp. 1-12. ISBN: 978-0-12-370626-3

[28] Stuart Chapin F, Matson PA, Vitousek PM. Principles of Terrestrial Ecosystem Ecology: Principles of Terrestrial Ecosystem Ecology. New York: Springer; 2012. pp. 1-529

[29] Hurwitz MM, Fleming EL, Newman PA, Li F, Mlawer E, Cady-Pereira K, et al. Ozone depletion by hydrofluorocarbons. Geophysical Research Letters. 2015;**42**(20):8686-8692. Available from: https://onlinelibrary.wiley.com/doi/full/10.1002/2015GL065856

[30] Schmidt U, Wetter T. Tropospheric chemistry and composition | H2. In: Encyclopedia of Atmospheric Sciences. Academic Press, Elsevier; 2003. pp. 2397-2403. ISBN: 978-0-12-227090-1

[31] Truhaut R. Ecotoxicology: Objectives, principles and perspectives. Ecotoxicology and Environmental Safety. 1977;**1**(2):151-173

[32] Sleeswijk AW, van Oers LFCM, Guinée JB, Struijs J, Huijbregts MAJ. Normalisation in product life cycle assessment: An LCA of the global and European economic systems in the year 2000. Science Total Environment. 2008;**390**(1):227-240

[33] Goedkoop MJ, Heijungs R, Huijbregts MAJ, De SA, Struijs J, van Zelm R. ReCiPe 2008 - a Life Cycle Impact Assessment Method Which Comprises Harmonised Category Indicators at the Midpoint and the Endpoint Level. The Netherlands: Ministry of Housing; 2013

[34] SimaPro. LCA Software for Informed-Change Makers: SimaPro. The Netherlands: Amersfoort; 2023. Available from: https://simapro.com/

[35] Sphera. Life Cycle Assessment Product Sustainability Software. Chicago: GaBi; 2023. Available from: https://sphera.com/life-cycle-assessment-lca-software/

[36] iPoint. Life Cycle Assessment (LCA) Software. Hamburg: Umberto; 2023. Available from: https://www.ifu.com/umberto/lca-software/

[37] One Click LCA. Building Life Cycle Assessment Software - One Click LCA. Helsinki, Finland; 2023 Available from: https://www.oneclicklca.com/

[38] OpenLCA. Open Source Life Cycle Assessment Software: OpenLCA. Berlin, Germany; 2023 Available from: https://www.openlca.org/

[39] Ghisellini P, Ripa M, Ulgiati S. Exploring environmental and economic costs and benefits of a circular economy approach to the construction and demolition sector. A literature review. Journal of Cleaned Products. 2018;(20):618-643

[40] Beermann K, Austin MC. An inspection of the life cycle of sustainable construction projects: Towards a biomimicry-based road map integrating circular economy. Biomimetics. 2021;**6**:67 Available from: https://www.mdpi.com/2313-7673/6/4/67/htm

[41] Sustainable Construction Technologies. Sustainable Construction Technologies. India: Butterworth-Heinemann, Elsevier; 2019. ISBN: 978-0-12-811749-1

[42] Braulio-Gonzalo M, Jorge-Ortiz A, Bovea MD. How are indicators in green building rating systems addressing sustainability dimensions and life cycle frameworks in residential buildings? Environmental Impact Assessment Review. 2021;**2022**(95):106793

[43] Cao C. 21 - sustainability and life assessment of high strength natural fibre composites in construction. In: Advanced High Strength Natural Fibre Composites in Construction. Woodhead Publishing, Elsevier Ltd; 2017. p. 529-544. ISBN: 978-0-08-100411-1

[44] Zanni S, Awere E, Bonoli A. Life Cycle Sustainability Assessment: An Ongoing Journey. Life Cycle

Sustainability Assessment for Decision-Making: Methodologies and Case Studies. India: Elsevier Inc.; 2020. p. 57-93. ISBN: 978-0-12-818355-7

[45] Benyus JM. Biomimicry: Innovation Inspired by Nature. 1st ed. New York: Morrow; 1997. p. 308

[46] Terrier P, Glaus M, Raufflet E. BiomiMETRIC assistance tool: A quantitative performance tool for biomimetic design. Biomimetics. 2019;**4**(3):1-19

[47] Helms M, Vattam SS, Goel AK. Biologically inspired design: Process and products. Design Studies. 2009;**30**(5):606-622

[48] Lv Q, Dqg O, Fruehwirth S, Development LI. LIVING envelope. WIT Transactions on Ecology and the Environment. 2008;**113**. p. 57-68

[49] Phoya S. Sustainable construction sites in Tanzania: Contractors' practices and their perspectives. International Journal of Construct Engineering Management. 2018;7(2):88-96. Available from: Sustainability is initially described as a desire to carry out activities without depleting resources or having harmful impacts on the environment. However, there is limited knowledge on how this desire is implemented by contractors in construction sites

[50] Tam CM, Tam VWY, Tsui WS. Green construction assessment for environmental management in the construction industry of Hong Kong. International Journal of Project Management. 2004;**22**(7):563-571

[51] Badarnah KL. Towards the LIVING Envelope: Biomimetics for Building Envelope Adaptation [Internet]. Delft, Netherlands: TUDelft, Delft University of Technology; 2012. Available from: http://resolver.tudelft.nl/uuid:4128b611-9b48-4c8d-b52f-38a59ad5de65. ISBN: 9789462032002

[52] Innovation Inspired by Nature — AskNature [Internet]. [cited 2022 Nov 28]. Available from: https://asknature.org/

[53] Meex E, Hollberg A, Knapen E, Hildebrand L, Verbeeck G. Requirements for applying LCA-based environmental impact assessment tools in the early stages of building design. Building and Environment. 2018;**133**:228-236

[54] de Pauw I, Kandachar P, Karana E, Peck D, Wever R. Nature inspired design: Strategies towards sustainability. In: Knowledge Collaboration & Learning for Sustainable Innovation: 14th European Roundtable on Sustainable Consumption and Production (ERSCP) conference and the 6th Environmental Management for Sustainable Universities (EMSU). Delft, Netherlands: TUDelft; 2023. Available from: https://repository.tudelft.nl/islandora/object/uuid%3A98ce3f26-eff8-40f5-82dc-ed92fec7e8f9

[55] Mcelroy MW, Jorna RJ, Van Engelen J. Sustainability quotients and the social footprint. Corp Society Responsibble Environment Management. 2008;**15**(4):223-234. Available from: https://onlinelibrary.wiley.com/doi/full/10.1002/csr.164

Chapter 4

Life-Cycle Assessment as a Next Level of Transparency in Denim Manufacturing

Sedef Uncu Akı, Cevza Candan, Banu Nergis and Neslihan Sebla Önder

Abstract

Increased consumer awareness and new regulations about climate change accelerated the need for solid, provable, transparent actions leading to results to support the sustainability claims and initiatives of fashion brands. However, progress on transparency is still very limited despite the alarming signals of climate change. As stated in Fashion Revolution's Transparency Index 2023, brands have achieved an overall average score of 24%, up 1% from last year. Transparency is a tool for transformation. A productive conversation toward the targets can only start with a certain level of transparency to lead to the desired change. Life cycle assessment (LCA) methodology represents the next level of transparency. LCA can help brands collect, analyze and monitor their sustainability performance with science-based results. It is a tool that is used to quantify the environmental performance of a product taking the complete life cycle into account (from raw material production to transport, fabric production, garment manufacturing, consumer use, and final disposal. This book chapter focuses on how brands can use LCA as a transparency tool, its advantages and challenges in generalizing the science-based data. A framework will be generated on how to build the LCA model and use the data to compare different products and production practices in denim industry.

Keywords: life cycle assessment, transparency, denim, environmental impact categories, sustainability, emissions

1. Introduction

As UN Secretary-General António Guterres said at Conference of the Parties (COP) on November 20th, 2022, the world should take more action to drastically reduce emissions immediately [1]. Unfortunately, action to transform the business practices continues to stay incremental, including the ones in the fashion industry. According to the Business of Fashion Sustainability Index 2022, the biggest players in the industry are still moving too slowly to achieve the set targets by 2030 [2]. Fashion brands need to measure their social and environmental impact continuously and act vigorously to decrease them. Consumer communication remains vital in this process with a certain level of transparency to lead to the desired change. However, "Green Washing" appears as a threat to real action as marketing activities without any solid and provable data become common practices for many brands in the fashion industry.

Life cycle assessment (LCA) methodology serves as a solution to "Green Washing" and represents the next level of transparency since LCA can help brands collect, analyze and monitor their sustainability performance with science-based results. Sustainable fibers and certified materials occur to be the most important choice for brands who would like to have green claims [3]. Although materials represent a significant role in the calculation of overall environmental impact of the products, other input and process parameters also are important in the overall calculation.

This chapter addresses the impact of the textile industry and processes, and the denim-related LCA studies first. It, then, offers a framework on how to build an LCA model in denim fabric manufacturing and use data to compare different products and production practices in this very industry.

2. Textile industry and its environmental impact

The global textile industry generates notable environmental impacts through the phases of raw material production, fiber, yarn and garment manufacturing, and garment use. The rise of global population and improved living standards have resulted in consistent increase in the production and consumption of textiles and fibers in the past few decades. According to the Global Fashion Industry Statistics, the world population was 7.84 billion in 2021 [4]. Despite the fact that the global apparel and footwear market has been affected by the COVID-19 pandemic and shrunk to $1.45 billion by −18.1% in 2020, the industry grew by 18% in 2020–2021, to $1.71 billion dollars. The global apparel retail market is expected to witness a 7.5% growth in 2021–2022 period and a 6.1% growth in 2022–2023 period.

Textiles generally count on petrochemical products, and fashion accounts for up to 10% of global carbon dioxide output. Polyester, which is a form of plastic derived from oil, has experienced an explosive growth and overtaken cotton in the textile production. Garments made from synthetic fibers such as polyester are the main prime source of microplastic pollution, which harms mainly the marine life [5, 6]. In Europe, clothing is the 4th most environment polluting category after food, housing, and transport industries. The way people dispose unwanted clothes has also changed, and about 87% of the total fibers used for clothing are ultimately incinerated or sent to a landfill. Only a small fraction is recycled. Fashion brands either destroy unsold products or send piles of them to landfills across the Global South.

2.1 Estimating the environmental impact of textile processing

In order to identify the environmental impacts caused by the long supply chain of textiles and to control them, there are various environmental standards applicable to textile products. This environmental information is related to the life cycle of a product and to each step of its manufacturing line. There are many important concepts related to environmental sustainability, and life cycle assessment (LCA) is the most important and common technique for assessing the overall environmental impact of a product, process, or service [7]. LCA is based on the ISO standards 14,040:2006 and ISO 14044:2018, which outline the processes required to carry out the study [8–10].

LCA comprises four major phases, as defined by ISO, which are [11].

1. definition of goal and scope,

2. life cycle inventory (LCI) analysis,

3. life cycle impact assessment (LCIA)

4. life cycle interpretation

The analyses require collection of data of the inventory substances, the emissions, and resources, involved in the product life cycle and are performed using specific software tools with;

data provided directly from companies and/or collected through audits;

data gathered from previous studies (LCA studies, literature); and

data from databases such as Ecoinvent, ELCD [12].

The effects of resources consumed and emissions released are detailed in the LCIA step which comprises the selection of impact categories such as depletion of abiotic resources, climate change, human toxicity, acidification, eutrophication, ecotoxicity, photo-oxidant formation, stratospheric ozone depletion, land use, water depletion, depletion of minerals, and use of fossil fuels. There are two different approaches to derive characterization factors namely, midpoint and endpoint approaches. In the midpoint approach, category impacts are translated into environmental topics such as climate change, acidification, water use, fossil depletion, freshwater eutrophication, etc. In the endpoint approach, the indicators are grouped into damage categories, including resources, ecosystems, and human health.

The midpoint indicators are calculated based on the data of relevant inventory data. The endpoint, on the other hand, assesses the environmental impact tracking to the end of the impact chain. Environmental impact indicators of LCA method are given in **Figure 1** [12].

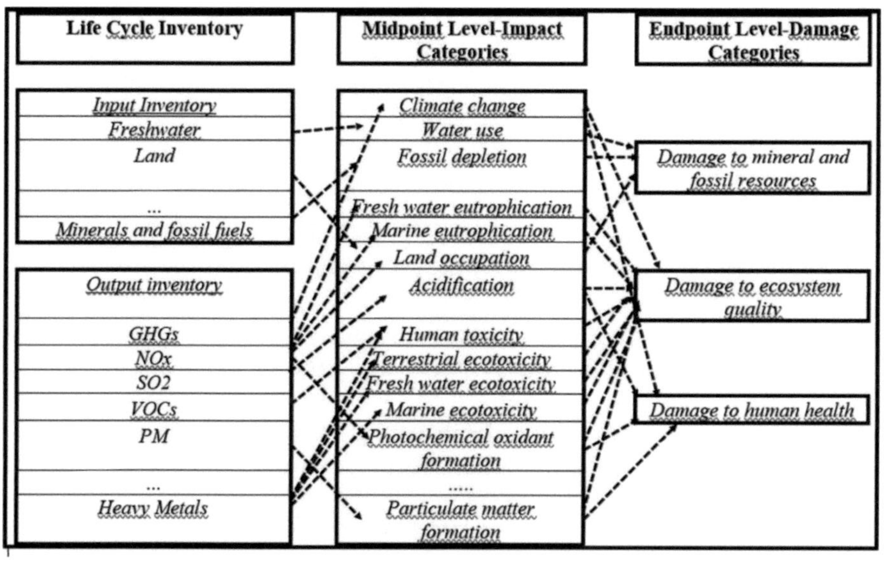

Figure 1.
Environmental impact indicators of LCA (as adopted from [12]).

A number of methods are available to quantify life cycle impacts [7, 13]. ReCiPe is one of the most recent and updated impact assessment methods available to LCA users. The method addresses 18 environmental concerns at the midpoint level and then collects the midpoints into a set of three endpoint categories [14]. CML method, created by the University of Leiden in the Netherlands in 2001, is a database that contains characterization factors for life cycle impact assessment (LCIA) [15]. The method is divided into baseline and non-baseline characterization methods, the former being the most common impact categories used in LCA. The impact assessment method implemented as CML-IA methodology is defined for the midpoint approach. In LIME-3 methodology, there are nine impact categories (climate change, air pollution, photochemical oxidants creation, water consumption, land use, mineral resource consumption, fossil fuel consumption, forest resource consumption, and solid waste) and four endpoints (human health, social assets, biodiversity, and primary production) for characterization. The conjoint analysis for weighting was conducted in all G20 countries [16]. TRACI is another environmental impact assessment tool that provides characterization factors for LCIA, industrial ecology, and sustainability metrics. The potential impacts of inputs and releases on specific impact categories are quantified in common equivalence units. Ozone depletion, climate change, acidification, eutrophication, smog formation, human health impacts, and ecotoxicity are the included impact categories in TRACI.

Resource uses of fossil fuels are also characterized [17]. For the characterization of human and ecotoxicological impacts of chemicals USEtox model, endorsed by UNEP's (the United Nations Environment Program) Life Cycle Initiative, provides midpoint and endpoint characterization factors for human toxicological and freshwater ecotoxicological impacts of chemical emissions in life cycle assessment. Main output is a database of characterization factors including exposure, effecting parameters, etc. [18]. A free web-based biodiversity broadcasting tool, BioScope, calculates the biodiversity footprint of products, companies, and investments provides businesses and financial institutions with a fast and simple indication of the main impacts their supply chains and financial products have on biodiversity [19].

These methods are linked to the software programs used in LCA. LCA software packages calculate the potential environmental impacts in a transparent way, based on inventory data. However, depending on the activity, whether the software has access to the right database needs to be checked. The differences among LCA softwares are categorized by Bach based on the following [20, 21]:

1. The origin: Broad variety of available LCA software programs are grouped regarding the developer, country of origin, and year of publication.

2. User knowledge: LCA software tools are designed for users who have no previous knowledge of LCA, who have basic knowledge, and for expert users.

3. Data source: Use of a predefined database that cannot be changed, or use of different databases that are open to software programs.

4. Entry format: Mass- and volume-related input data can be supplied in spreadsheet or geometric-based format.

5. Optimization: Optimization can either be conducted manually or computationally.

6. Default settings: Provide a basic structure to ease the applicability and execution of the LCA for the user. In some programs, default settings are introduced to simplify and speed up the execution of the LCA.

7. Life cycle phases: In general, LCA is divided into three groups of life cycle phases as production, use phase, and end-of-life. A distinction is made between three levels such that some programs consider only part of the production process while others also include part of the deconstruction and recycling process, and some consider parts of all life cycle phases.

A set of criteria for qualitative comparison of LCA software tools was also presented by Silva et.al as; software origin and version, dataset format, user interface, LCA result presentation, uncertainty/sensitivity analysis of results, support facilities for users, positive and negative modeling aspects, and other relevant aspects [22].

SimaPro, GaBi, Umberto, and Open-LCA are some of the most popular and widely known tools used for LCA. A broad list of tools is available in the LCA resources directory of the European Commission's website [23]. GaBi and Simapro programs were introduced in the early 90s and are regarded as the earliest softwares. Following them, Umberto was developed to address material assessment. Today, the softwares have evolved into LCA expert tools based on elaborate information [24–27]. The topics covered by different LCA softwares are diverse and it is important to consider the particularities of the softwares when selecting an appropriate LCA tool.

In a study conducted in order to assess whether the use of different softwares namely, SimaPro and GaBi, can cause a difference for the LCA results used for modeling a product system or doing an impact assessment, differences were identified in particular for the implementation of the impact assessment methods. It appeared that the observed differences came primarily from differences/errors in the different databases of the softwares [28].

In another study in which a gate-to-gate product system (particleboards production in Brazil) was assessed with the same functional unit using GaBi, openLCA, SimaPro, and Umberto NXT, the modeling principles, hotspots, and impacts for each software tool compared in. Acidification, climate change, ecotoxicity, human toxicity, and photochemical ozone formation from the ILCD/PEF method were the selected midpoint impact categories. It was identified that up to 22.7% more impacts were calculated by SimaPro to acidification, and up to 66.7% more impacts to photochemical ozone formation than compared to other software tools. Thus, depending on the software tool a user chooses, LCA results showed variations [22]. LCA software tools are also widely used for textile products.

3. An overview of denim-related life cycle assessment (LCA) studies

The global denim jeans market is expected to reach almost $60 billion in 2023. Besides, it is well known that the entire lifecycle of one pair of denim jeans has a significant environmental impact so far as the world's ecological balance is concerned. As a result, with the effect of increasing consumer awareness, denim industry has shifted toward adopting more sustainable manufacturing processes, which in turn makes it necessary more than ever for the industry to systematically evaluate the environmental impacts of denim fabric production from a life cycle perspective in an attempt to effectively handle consumer related activities.

Despite the sizeable consumption of denim garments, there are very limited studies regarding LCA of such products. Levi Strauss and Co. was one of the first brands conducting an LCA to analyze the environmental impact of a pair of Levi jeans for its entire life span. Their study indicated that about 3781 L of freshwater was consumed and 33.4 kg CO2 eq of greenhouse gas (GHG) was emitted throughout the entire lifespan of a pair of cotton jeans. Moreover, it showed that consumer care had the largest impact (37%) on climate change over the life cycle, which was followed by the fabric product (27%) [29].

Hackett et al. studied the cradle-to-gate phases of the life cycle assessment of a pair of denim jeans and a T-shirt utilizing ReCiPe 2008 methodology. The study demonstrated that cotton fiber cultivation and harvesting most significantly contributed to the overall environmental impacts, and that the use of fertilizers, pesticides, and irrigation water had a direct influence on this very impact [30].

Karthik and Murugan studied carbon foot print (CF) values for all activities involved in manufacturing denim and identified the relevant processes and technologies contributing most to greenhouse gases (GHG) emissions [31].

Vos performed a water footprint (WF) assessment on a pair of blue jeans using a hybrid approach of the LCA and water footprint assessment (WFA) methods. The results revealed that raw materials (64%) and consumer washing (32%) dominated the blue WF [32].

Morita et al. in their study, investigated the environmental (climate changes [CC]) and energy performance (primary energy demand [PED]) of jeans manufacture in Brazil using LCA method. They found that CC and PED impacts associated with the production of one pair of jeans were 7.86 kg CO_2 eq and 124 MJ, respectively. Moreover, they proposed scenarios based on cotton and yarn imports as well as jeans themselves from the United States, in addition to the replacement of natural gas for wood. They demonstrated that the decreased impact of CC (4.44 kg CO_2 eq/FU) belongs to the production of jeans in Brazil using wood for heating [33].

Akı et al. conducted an experimental work regarding the life cycle assessment of a denim fabric with and without recycled fiber content using SimaPro software as assessment tool and the inventory based on denim production figures of a denim company in Turkey. They concluded that global warming potential decreases by 5%, eutrophication drops by 8% and abiotic resource depletion by 3% with each addition of 10% recycled content in the fiber blend used for denim production. In their following study, the authors mapped and discussed the environmental impact of recycled and bio-based polymeric fibers in a denim fabric using LCA as a framework. In doing so, the methodology given in the authors' previous study was employed and all of the calculations were performed from cradle to denim factory gate. Furthermore, the inventory was based on the 2020 denim production figures of a denim company in Turkey. The results indicated that Tencel and Refibra scored the lowest in every impact category analyzed, except for the land use. They also showed that PLA appeared to have better values in every environmental impact category, when compared to PET, though recycled PET performed better than PLA for Global Warming Potential, Eutrophication and Abiotic Depletion impacts [34, 35].

Zhao et al. analyzed the virtual carbon and water flows in the global denim-product trade using the footprint methods. The findings of the study indicated that virtual carbon in the global denim trade increased from 14.8 Mt. CO_2e in 2001 to 16.0 Mt. CO_2e in 2018 whereas the virtual water consumption decreased from 5.6 billion m^3 in 2001 to 4.7 billion m^3 in 2018. Moreover, the results revealed that both the denim fabric and cotton fiber production contributed the most of the carbon emissions and water consumption, and that polyester blended denim had 5% greater carbon footprint and 72% lower water footprint than its cotton counterpart [36].

Fidan et al. performed an integrated sustainability assessment of denim fabric made from mechanically recycled cotton fiber by applying combined heat and power plant (CHP) for fabric production. In that study, global warming potential (GWP), acidification potential (AP), eutrophication potential (EP), water use, and cumulative energy demand (CED) were taken as environmental impact categories, and accordingly, the LCA results revealed that the highest environmental impact improvements were obtained as 98% water use, 90%EP, 74% AP, 63% CED, and 54% GWP when 100% recycled cotton and CHP plant were used in the production [37]. Fidan et al., in another study did investigate the benefits of organic cotton fiber use in denim production with the help of life cycle assessment methodology based on four different scenarios. The environmental impact categories of global warming potential, eutrophication, terrestrial ecotoxicity, acidification, and freshwater ecotoxicity potential were analyzed using CML-IA method. The results showed that the lowest environmental impacts were obtained when 100% organic cotton fiber (scenario 4) was employed as raw material, such that it improved terrestrial ecotoxicity and freshwater ecotoxicity potential by 87% and 59%, respectively [38].

Luo et al. extended the LCA research boundary to the entire life cycle of textile products by adopting the process-level modular water footprint (WF) assessment method proposed by Li et al. [39] into both carbon and water footprints assessment of textile products. In doing so, the key issues such as module decomposition based on complex process flows and technology options, together with assembly methodology of process modules in varying product life cycle stages, were taken into account. They accordingly utilized a case study of a pair of cotton jeans to verify the feasibility as well as flexibility of the method. The results of the study revealed that the greenhouse (GHG) emissions, water consumption, water eutrophication and water eco toxicity impacts for the life cycle of one pair of jeans from cotton cultivation to product disposal were 90.37 kg CO2 eq, 13.74 m3 H2O eq, 1.67×10^{-2} kg PO_4^{3-} eq and 112.41 m3 H2O eq, respectively, and that finishing, cotton cultivation and laundering processes were major contributors to the environmental impacts under discussion. Finally, the study proposed 12 scenarios based on the Chinese consumers' care patterns, which pointed out that the washing with top loader washing machine, line drying, and no ironing once a month in 2-year lifetime of jeans was the best combination by contributing 1.86%, 4.86%, 19.00%, and 1.08% to the total CF, WSF, water eutrophication footprint, and water ecotoxicity footprint, in turn [40].

The existing studies on LCA analysis of denim products (fabrics, garments), majority of which focuses on cotton based denim, imply that the scope of researches may be broadened toward the works on both renewable resources and recycling of materials to see the sustainability rate of a product.

4. Building a life cycle assessment (LCA) model for denim fabric manufacturing

The motivation or the reason for doing denim LCA helps practitioners to structure their LCA model. The main framework for LCA studies is ISO 14040/44 standards [8, 9]. In addition, the communication way or tool of LCA study is also a determinative indicator for the construction of LCA study for such as determining the functional unit and the scope and/or system boundary of the study. A denim fabric mill can perform a cradle to gate LCA study including the production of raw materials, transport of all materials to a factory, production steps and packaging of the final fabric or a gate-to-gate study to cover only production stages of the fabric.

Following an Environmental Product Declaration (EPD) format is another way of constructing an LCA study and communicating its results. Defined by ISO 14025, an EPD document is an ISO type III Environmental Declaration that reports comparable and third-party verified data about products and services' environmental performances from a lifecycle perspective [41]. EPDs are registered in the framework of a program and the study behind of an EPD is constructed according to these programs' Product Category Rules (PCR) guidelines and rules. The International EPD® System is one of the framework programs used for EPD construction and registration [42].

In the following sections, constructing a LCA model for denim fabric will be explained via a case study based on the production practices of denim fabrics by a Turkish denim mill.

4.1 Defining a functional unit/declared unit

One of the fundamental steps of product LCA's is to define functional unit of the study. The selling unit for denim fabric is meters or yards depending on the market geography. The weight of the denim fabric is, on the other hand, communicated in oz./yd^2 or gr/m^2 units. And the width of the fabric determines how garment manufacturers place their cutting patterns on fabric and minimize their cutting waste and use optimum amount of fabrics. Therefore, using a weight unit as a functional unit in a fabric LCA is not feasible.

The PCR for the fabrics states that a declared unit for fabrics should be used instead of a functional unit as the fabrics are intermediate products with many different potential uses and a functional unit cannot be defined from functional aspects of a fabric. Therefore, m^2 is used as the declared unit in fabric LCAs [43].

4.2 The scope and system boundary

As stated in Section 2.1, the scope of LCA studies are divided into four sections: cradle-to-gate (upstream), gate-to-gate(core), gate-to-grave(downstream) or cradle-to-grave which covers all of the steps in the lifecycle. Denim fabrics are intermediate products that can be used in many different garment styles with the application of different washes. And the use and the life span of the denim garment vary for individuals (consumers) depending on their lifestyle, culture, geography, etc. This makes the construction of the use phase life cycle stage of a denim fabric very complicated and scenario-based.

Therefore, a fabric mill can choose to practice a cradle-to-gate LCA for their products covering the upstream processes including the production of raw materials and packaging materials and core processes including all relevant transport down to factory gate, energy, and water consumption during manufacturing operations by the denim mill including spinning, warping, sizing, weaving, finishing, rolling, and packaging processes (cradle-to-gate).

A representation of the system boundary of a cradle-to-gate and cradle-to-grave denim fabric LCA and activities covered within is given in **Figure 2**.

If a mill chooses to proceed with an EPD, the PCR should be followed when defining the system boundary. The life cycle stages with the relative modules are given in

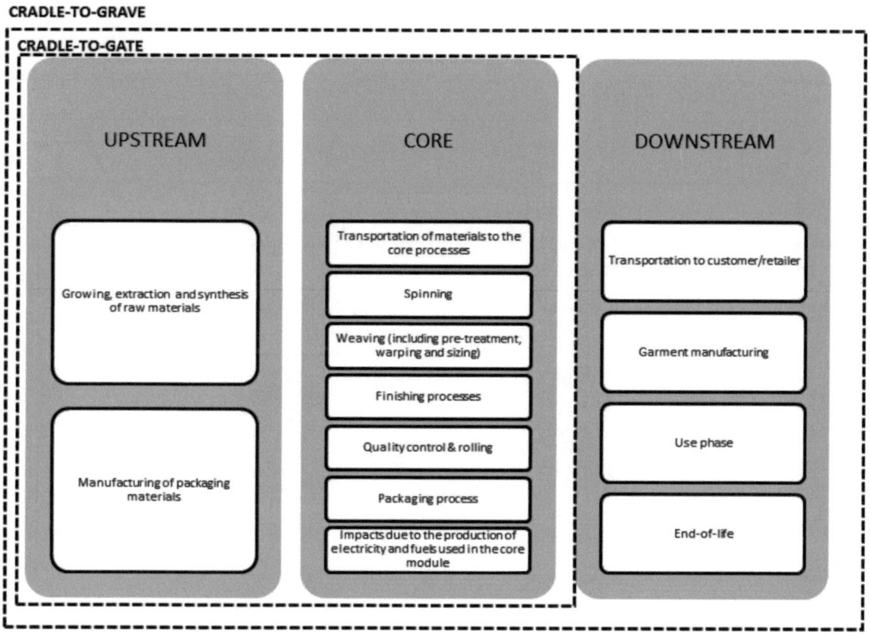

Figure 2.
System boundary of the LCA study.

Table 1. In line with the system boundary, for EPDs the calculation procedure should also be separated into three life cycle stages as upstream processes (cradle-to-gate), core processes (gate-to-gate), and downstream processes (gate-to-grave) and shall be reported as such [43].

4.3 Life cycle inventory (LCI) and "data"/"background data" quality

Primary or site-specific and secondary data is used in LCAs. Primary data are those collected directly from the production site relevant to the life cycle stages modeled. If there is no primary data available, then data from the LCI databases are used as secondary data.

Apart from environmental impacts from upstream supply chain of raw materials production, all production data are collected from production lines with reference to a base year. A general practice is to use average data of at least 1 year of a recent production period per declared unit production and should reflect actual production at the specific location.

Necessary background data (secondary data) relevant to life cycle stages are taken from the databases. While no guidelines indicate a timeframe or recommendations for databases, it is a good practice to share the versions and date of database releases used in the background study with the communication of the results.

4.4 Life cycle impact analysis (LCIA) methods

One of the most important parts of an LCA is the outputs. With a Life Cycle Analysis software, SimaPro, for example, it is possible to calculate many impacts via a number of impact assessment methods [44].

Life cycle stage	Life cycle module	Life cycle module group	Mandatory/optional
Upstream	A1) Raw material supply	A1–A3) Product stage	Mandatory
	A2) Transport		Mandatory
Core	A3) Manufacturing		Mandatory
Downstream	A4) Transportation of the fabric to retailer	A4–A5) Forming stage	Optional
	A5) Further processing of the fabric		Optional
	B1) Transportation of the fabric to the use phase	B1–B2) Use stage	Optional
	B2) Use of the fabric by the consumer		Optional
	C1) Disassembling/ sorting	C1–C3) End-of-life stage	Mandatory (but may be excluded for fabric if specific criteria are met)
	C2) Transport to recovery/disposal		Mandatory (but may be excluded for fabric if specific criteria are met)
	C3) Final disposal		Mandatory (but may be excluded for fabric if specific criteria are met)

Table 1.
The life cycle module groups according to PCR for fabrics [43].

The mill that is currently taken into consideration as the case study reviewed the industry guidelines and standards to determine which environmental impacts to focus on for their LCA studies. After scanning process, 5 impact categories were chosen to be assessed. These impacts, their definitions and calculation methodologies within the SimaPro 9.0.0 software are given in **Table 2**.

For EPDs, PCR documents guide the LCA practitioner on impact analysis. Defined in the PCR for fabrics, the calculated environmental impacts and inventory indicators should be separated into three life cycle stages as upstream processes (cradle-to-gate), core processes (gate-to-gate), and downstream processes (gate-to-grave) and shall be reported as such. The environmental impact indicators that should be declared in EPDs and the calculation methodologies are described in the EPD program website [43, 50].

For example, the environmental impact indicator Global Warming Potential should be calculated for each life cycle module stated in **Table 1** in terms of fossil, biogenic, land use and land transformation and as total by using the calculation method GWP100, EN 15804. Version: August 2021 as stated in the program website as shown in **Table 3** [50].

In addition to the environmental impact categories, use of resources, output flows and waste categories are declared in EPD documents per declared unit for each life cycle stage according to the relevant PCR guidelines [43]. The use of resources and output flows and waste categories are given in **Tables 4** and **5**, respectively.

Impact category	Unit	Description	Example impact	Calculation method within SimaPro 9.0.0
Global Warming Potential	kg CO_2 eq	Emission of greenhouse gases (GHGs)	Climate change	IPCC 2013 GWP 100a: methodology developed by the Intergovernmental Panel on Climate Change [45]
Freshwater use	lt	Freshwater taken from the environment	Excessive use leads to water scarcity	LCA inventory data
Land use	m^2a	The amount of agricultural area occupied	Deforestation	ReCiPe 2016 midpoint method: created by RIVM, Radboud University, Norwegian University of Science and Technology and PRé Consultants [46, 47]
Eutrophication potential	kg PO_4^{3-} eq	Emission of substances to water contributing to oxygen depletion	Nutrient loading to stream – water pollution	CML-IA baseline methodology: LCA methodology developed by the Center of Environmental Science (CML) of Leiden University in The Netherlands [48, 49]
Abiotic Resource depletion	kg Sb eq	Measure of mineral, metal and fossil fuel resources used to produce a product	Mineral scarcity	CML-IA baseline methodology (version 3.05, updated on November 2017): LCA methodology developed by the Center of Environmental Science (CML) of Leiden University in The Netherlands [48, 49]

Table 2.
Selected environmental impact categories for the case study.

Parameter		Unit	Upstream		Core
			A1) Raw material supply	A2) Transport	A3) Manufacturing
Global Warming (GWP100a)	Fossil	kg CO_2 eq	—	—	—
	Biogenic		—	—	—
	Land use and land transformation		—	—	—
	Total		—	—	—

Table 3.
LCA results framework for Global Warming (GWP100a) indicator with mandatory life cycle stages and modules [50].

5. An environmental impact assessment framework for denim fabrics

There are five main steps in product development that affect the sustainability score of a denim fabric:

a. Elasticity of the denim fabric

b. Weight of the denim fabric

Parameter		Unit
Primary energy resources, renewable	Use as energy carrier	MJ, net calorific value
	Use as raw materials	MJ, net calorific value
	Total	MJ, net calorific value
Primary energy resources, non-renewable	Use as energy carrier	MJ, net calorific value
	Use as raw materials	MJ, net calorific value
	Total	MJ, net calorific value
Secondary material		kg
Renewable secondary fuels		MJ, net calorific value
Non-renewable secondary fuels		MJ, net calorific value
Net use of fresh water		m^3

Table 4.
Use of resources per declared unit.

Parameter	Unit
Hazardous waste disposed (HWD)	kg
Non-Hazardous waste disposed (NHWD)	kg
Radioactive waste disposed (RWD)	kg
Components for reuse (CRU)	kg
Material for recycling (MFR)	kg
Materials for energy recovery (MER)	kg
Exported energy, electricity	MJ
Exported energy, thermal	MJ

Table 5.
Output flows and waste categories.

c. Composition of the denim fabric

d. Dyeing method of the denim fabric

e. Finish of the denim fabric

Product developers and/or designers in brands decide for each step to construct the desired look. This decision also determines the environmental impact of the fabric (**Table 6**). An environmental impact assessment framework for different types of denim fabrics is developed based on an LCA model to use scientific data to compare different products and production practices in denim industry (**Figure 3**).

Accordingly, the details of the five main steps in product development that are influential on the sustainability score of a denim fabric is given as follows:

Choose your denim fabric's elasticity	Choose your denim fabric's weight	Choose your denim fabric's composition	Choose your denim fabric's dyeing method	Choose your denim fabric's finish
Rigid	Lightweight (6–10 oz)	100% cotton	Indigo	Standard
Comfort stretch	Midweight (10–12 oz)	100% organic cotton	Indigo flow	Sanfor
Bi-stretch	Heavyweight (12–16 oz)	Recycled cotton	Sulfur	Alchemy
Super stretch		Cotton rich – cellulosic blend	Sulfur Top/ Bottom	I-core
		Cotton rich – synthetic blend	Reactive	Coating
		ZERO-MAX®	Ready to dye/ NTE	Overdye
				Flat optic
				Natural finish
				Optic finish
				Ready to dye

Table 6.
Five main steps in the framework of the study.

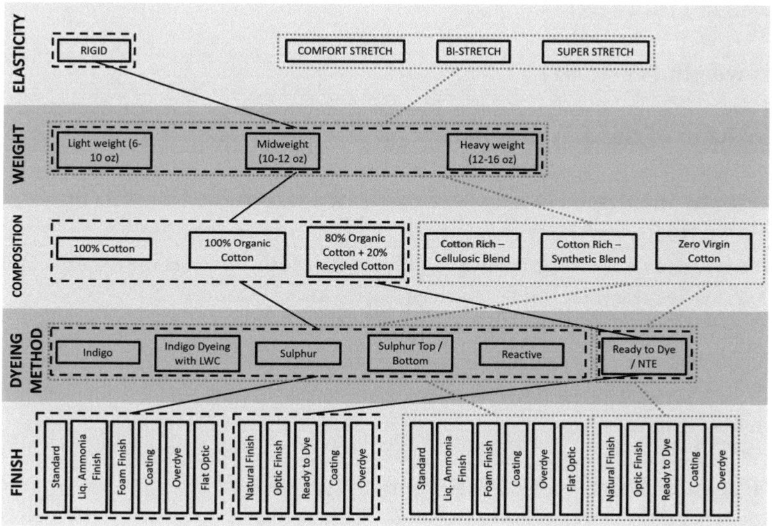

Figure 3.
An environmental impact assessment framework for denim fabrics.

5.1 Elasticity of the denim fabric

According to the elasticity of the denim fabric, the route of the production and process parameters change. This affects energy usage, water usage, waste and chemical usage, hence the selected environmental impacts. For denim fabrics, four stretch levels are used in the framework (**Figure 3**), namely:

- Rigid: 100% rigid denim fabric with no stretch property.
- Comfort Stretch: Denim fabric with up to 35% elasticity added for comfort.
- Super Stretch: Denim fabric with highly engineered constructions and stretching blends that achieves more than 35% stretch.
- Bi-stretch: Denim with elasticity, in both warp and weft direction, that offers slimming and sculpting effect to the wearer.

5.2 Weight of the denim fabric

Weight of the fabric determines the amount of raw material required. Primary and secondary data of the upstream processes are incorporated into the calculations as a weight unit, kg/oz. Hence, the selected impact category values differ based on the weight of the fabric. For denim fabrics, three categories are constructed into the framework (**Figure 3**).

- Lightweight (6–10 oz)
- Midweight (10–12 oz)
- Heavyweight (12–16 oz)

5.3 Composition of the denim fabric

Different raw materials; cotton, cellulosic or man-made fibers as input materials and data associated with these raw materials' production should be included in the calculations when cradle-to-gate approach is selected. Several blend alternatives are taken into consideration in the framework (**Figure 3**)

- 100% Cotton
- 100% Organic Cotton
- 80% Organic Cotton and 20% Recycled Cotton
- Cotton-rich and Cellulosic Fiber Blend: Denim fabric with cotton-rich composition, blended with cellulosic content, such as lyocell, viscose, and modal.
- Cotton-rich and Synthetic Fiber Blend: Denim fabric with cotton-rich composition, blended with synthetic content, such as polyester.

- Zero-Virgin Cotton: Denim fabric with no virgin cotton content that contains regenerated cellulosic fibers, recycled cotton, and synthetic fibers.

5.4 Warp dyeing method of the denim fabric

Warp dyeing methodology affects energy usage, water usage, waste and chemical usage during production, hence the magnitude of the selected environmental impacts (**Figure 3**).

- Indigo Dyeing: Conventional indigo warp dyeing process that produces conventional blue color and shade alike to blue color.

- Indigo Dyeing with less water consumption (LWC): This is a sustainable indigo dyeing process in which up to 70% water saving can be achieved.

- Reactive Dyeing: In reactive dyeing process, water-soluble reactive dyes form strong covalent bonds with cellulosic fibers which result in good wash fastness. This requires different chemicals and process parameters than regular indigo dyeing.

- Sulfur Dyeing: In sulfur dyeing process, sulfur dyestuff which is a form of vat dyes (water insoluble dye) is applied through chemical reduction process. This dyeing process is commonly used for dark shades such as black, navy, brown, khaki, and green.

- Sulfur Top/Bottom Dyeing: Sulfur top dyeing is an application of sulfur dye after indigo dyeing. Sulfur bottom dyeing is an application of sulfur dye before indigo dyeing to decrease the amount of time needed to achieve deeper colors and obtaining a different cast.

5.5 Finish of the denim fabric

Finishing steps in denim fabric production are essential for the performance and appearance of the fabric. After weaving, fabric is mechanically and chemically treated to give it a soft hand feel, to correct the dimensional stability, to add a new shade or color on the original warp color or to add performance feature to the fabric (**Figure 3**).

- Standard Finish: Standard finish is the main process that involves removing the sizing agent from the fabric and adjusting the dimensional stability.

- Liquid Ammonia Finish: Alchemy is an eco-finishing process that adds softness as well as anti-pilling and wrinkle-free properties to denim while using about 90% of chemicals in close circuit and near zero water.

- Foam Finish: This finish process is an environmental-friendly sulfur and indigo coating. I-Core is a foam finishing process technology that achieves low chemical, water and energy use.

- Coating: This process covers the surface or back of denim fabric with chemicals and dyestuff in order to gain or improve various surface properties or to achieve a shade/cast on the original warp color.

- Overdye: Denim fabric is dyed in this process in finishing stage to achieve a shade/cast on the original warp color.

- Flat Optic Finish: This is a finish to achieve flat and lustrous look.

- Natural Finish: This is a finishing process for undyed denim fabric that involves removing the sizing agent from the fabric and adjusting the dimensional stability.

- Optic Finish: This is a finishing process which is applied to undyed denim fabric to achieve bright white color.

In the framework (**Figure 3**), the fabric compositions are accumulated to three different groups for each rigid and comfort/stretch elasticity levels. The impacts coming from fiber compositions are constructed according to the weight of fibers used in each composition group and weight level. The following production stages, namely spinning, warping, sizing, unwarping, weaving, packaging, and quality control, are taken as fixed processes for all design variations and based on 1 meter of fabric production. The impacts originated from dyeing and finishing processes are allocated according to the yearly production of 1 meter of dyed warp yarn and finishing of 1 meter of raw fabric, respectively, for each dyeing and finishing recipe.

Warp dyeing method of a denim fabric is independent from the raw material or elasticity choices. **Figure 4** shows the difference in the selected environmental impacts based on different warp dyeing methods. Regular indigo dyeing has the highest impact compared to the other methods in four categories-global warming

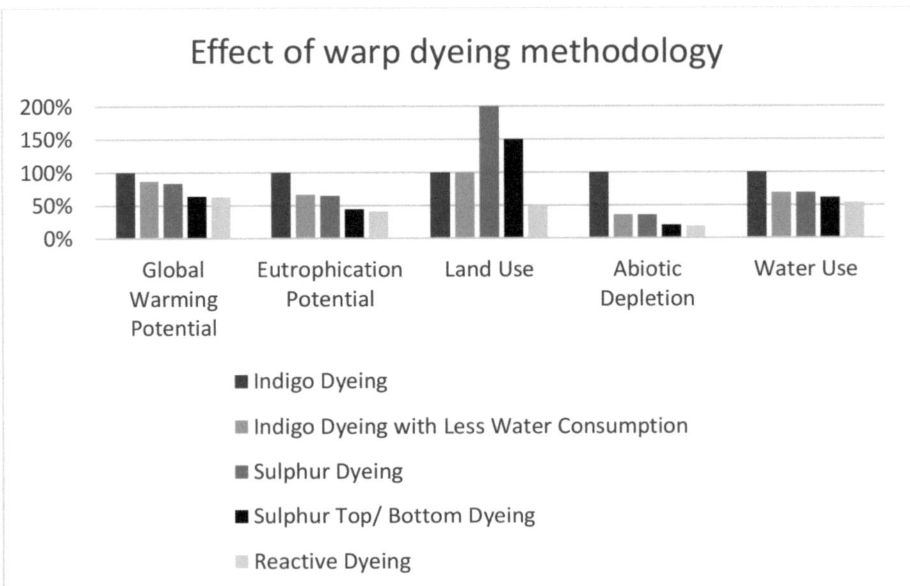

Figure 4.
Effect of warp dyeing methodology.

potential, eutrophication potential, abiotic depletion and water use out of five. In terms of land use, the environmental impact of sulfur dyes is almost doubled compared to indigo dyeing.

Figure 5 shows the difference in the selected environmental impacts based on different finishing processes of a denim fabric. Optic finish and i-core finish have the highest impact in all of the impact categories. Coating and overdyeing follow these finishes.

As may be seen from both **Figures 5** and **6**, percentages are used as a measure to compare the different methods, as the absolute values are in different scales for each impact category and for the relevant routes.

In the impact assessment for each indicator, the burden coming from each composition per different weights, warp dyeing methodologies and finishing processes is added on top of the impacts coming from the fixed processes. **Figure 6** is an example

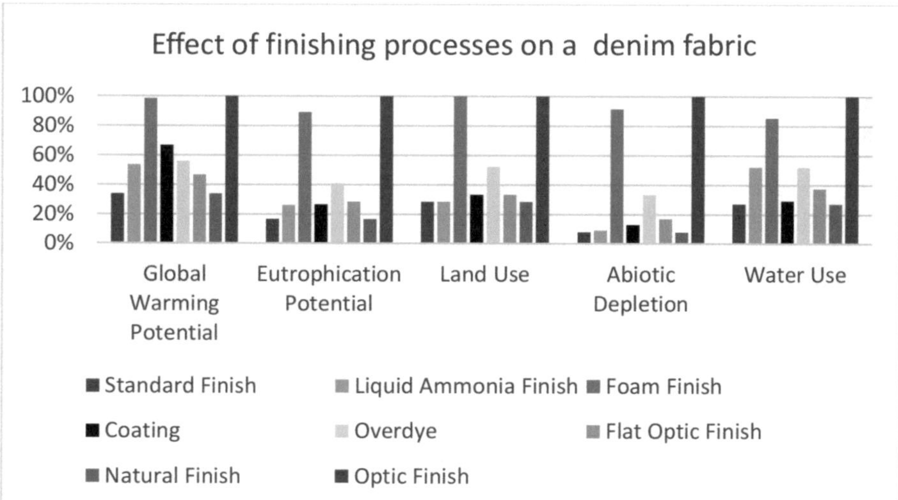

Figure 5.
Effect of finishing processes for a denim fabric.

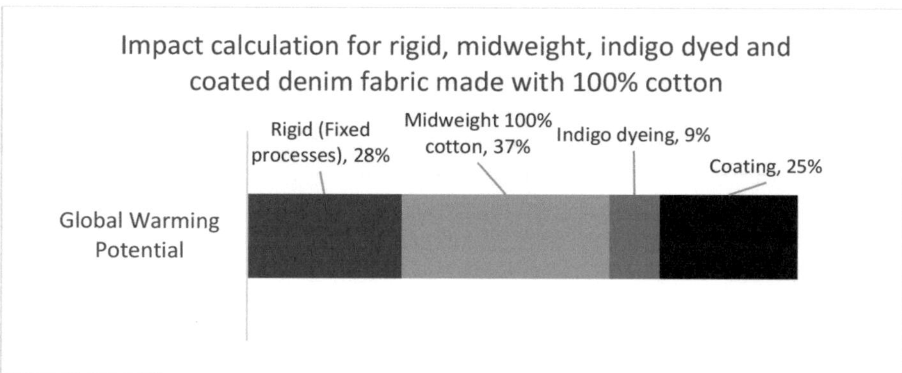

Figure 6.
An example of an impact calculation for rigid, mid-weight, indigo dyed, and coated denim fabric made with 100% cotton.

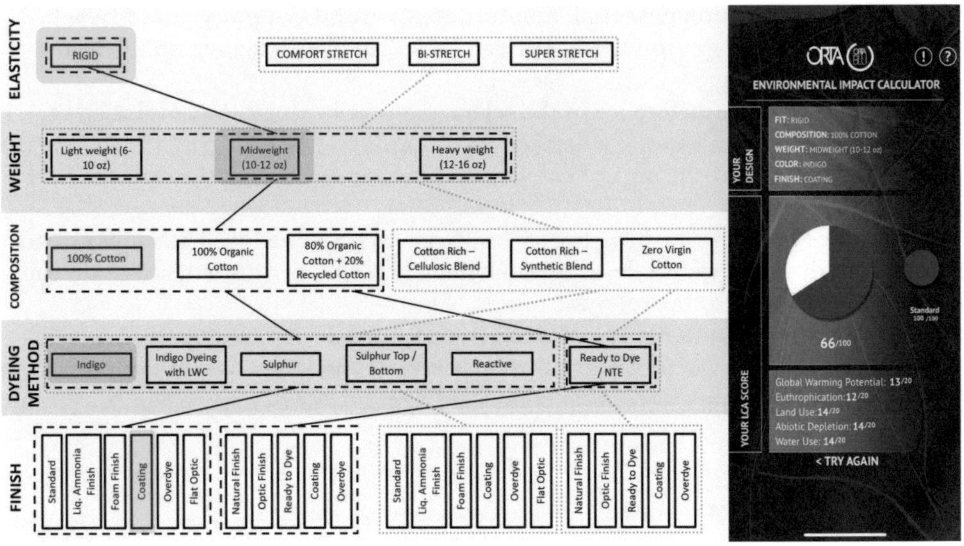

Figure 7.
An example of a route selection for rigid, mid-weight, indigo dyed, and coated denim fabric made with 100% cotton.

of the global warming potential calculation of a rigid, mid-weight, indigo dyed, and coated 100% cotton denim.

A comparison model can be developed for distinctive denim fabric designs based on normalizing and scoring each step in the LCA. Particular routes in the framework can be selected and results can be compared to a defined standard denim (**Figure 7**).

6. Conclusions

This chapter introduces an environmental impact assessment framework for denim fabrics. This framework provides an opportunity to calculate impacts of product developers' and/or designers' choices in defining the denim fabric they would like to develop using scientific LCA data. One can even compare the impact results of different types of denim fabrics without even producing the fabric itself. Calculating and sharing this detailed science-based data also represents a new level of transparency. On the contrary to the common belief of raw materials being the main impact generators in denim fabrics, the framework also proves that impacts occurred during denim fabric manufacturing, during the production of the raw and auxiliary materials, and impacts of the background processes should all be taken into consideration.

There are challenges in LCA calculations since the primary data is highly company-specific. Therefore, the chapter focused on normalizing the data and creating a scaling that can be used in decision-making.

Greenwashing is not only denims but today's one of the growing problems in every sector, in every product. Baseless claims and marketing statement caused this problem and now it is really hard to clean it up. Certifications and labels were seen as one of the solutions to this problem however, industry experiences misapplications during the certification process in the last couple of years. There is an information pollution in the market on what is sustainable denim. This framework will help designers/companies compare their choices about their sustainable denim fabric definitions via science-based data.

Conflict of interest

The authors declare no conflict of interest.

Author details

Sedef Uncu Akı[1], Cevza Candan[2*], Banu Nergis[2] and Neslihan Sebla Önder[1]

1 Orta Anadolu TAŞ, İstanbul, Turkey

2 Istanbul Technical University, İstanbul, Turkey

*Address all correspondence to: candance@itu.edu.tr

References

[1] United Nations: Climate action [Internet]. 2022. Available from: https://www.un.org/en/climatechange/cop27 [Accessed: February 5, 2023]

[2] Kent S. Business of Fashion Sustainability Index [Internet]. 2022. Available from: https://www.businessoffashion.com/articles/sustainability/widespread-inaction-on-sustainability-eclipses-progress-at-fashions-biggest-companies/ [Accessed: February 5, 2023]

[3] Bates V, Baumann-Pauly KD. Amplifiying misinformation: The case of sustainability indices in fashion [Internet]. 2023. Available from: https://www.veronicabateskassatly.com/read/amplifying-misinformation-the-case-of-sustainability-indices-in-fashion[Accessed: February 1, 2023]

[4] Fashion United. Global fashion industry statistics [Internet]. 2022. Available from: https://fashionunited.com/global-fashion-industry-statistics [Accessed: January 9, 2023]

[5]] Dottle R, Gu J. The global glut of clothing is an environmental crisis [Internet]. 2022. Available from: https://www.bloomberg.com/graphics/2022-fashion-industry-environmental-impact/ [Accessed: January 9, 2023]

[6] News European Parliament. The impact of textile production and waste on the environment [Internet]. 2020. Available from: https://www.europarl.europa.eu/news/en/headlines/society/20201208STO93327/the-impact-of-textile-production-and-waste-on-the-environment-infographic [Accessed: January 9, 2023]

[7] Muthu SS. Ways of measuring the environment. In: Muthu SS, Assessing the Environmental Impact of Textiles and the Clothing Supply Chain. 2nd ed. United Kingdom: Woodhead Publishing, Elsevier Ltd. 2017. pp. 34-56. ISBN: 978-0-12-819783-7

[8] International Organization for Standardization. [Internet]. 2006. Environmental management – life cycle assessment – principles and framework (ISO Standard No. 14040:2006). Available from: https://www.iso.org/standard/37456.html.

[9] International Organization for Standardization. [Internet]. 2006. Environmental management – life cycle assessment – requirements and guidelines (ISO Standard No. ISO 14044:2006 + Amd 2:2020). Available from: https://www.iso.org/standard/76122.html.

[10] Tedesco S, Montacchini E. From textile waste to resource: A methodological approach of research and experimentation. Sustainability. 2020;**12**:10667. DOI: 10.3390/su122410667

[11] Muthu SS. Estimating the overall environmental impact of textile processing: Life cycle assessment of textile products. In: Muthu SS, editor. Assessing the Environmental Impact of Textiles and the Clothing Supply Chain. 2nd ed. United Kingdom: Woodhead Publishing, Elsevier Ltd. 2017. pp. 105-129. ISBN: 978-0-12-819783-7

[12] Luo Y, Song K, Ding X, Wu X. Environmental sustainability of textiles and apparel: A review of evaluation methods. Environmental Impact Assessment Review. 2021;**86**:106497. DOI: 10.1016/j.eiar.2020.106497

[13] Balanay R, Halog A. Tools for circular economy: Review and some potential

applications for the Philippine textile industry. In: Muthu SS, editor. Circular Economy in Textiles and Apparel. 1st ed. United Kingdom: Elsevier Ltd; 2018. pp. 49-75. ISBN: 9780081026304

[14] Netherlands National Institute for Public Health and the Environment. Ministry of Health, Welfare and Sport. LCIA: The ReCiPe model [Internet]. 2018. Available from: https://www.rivm.nl/en/life-cycle-assessment-lca/recipe [Accessed: January 9, 2023]

[15] Universiteit Leiden. Tools and data overview of CML software and data [Internet]. 2023. Available from: https://www.universiteitleiden.nl/en/science/environmental-sciences/tools-and-data [Accessed: January 9, 2023]

[16] LCA Society of Japan. LIME Method [Internet]. 2018. Available from: https://lca-forum.org/english/lime/ [Accessed: January 16, 2023]

[17] US Environmental Protection Agency. Tool for reduction and assessment of chemicals and other environmental impacts (TRACI) [Internet]. 2022. Available from: https://www.epa.gov/chemical-research/tool-reduction-and-assessment-chemicals-and-other-environmental-impacts-traci [Accessed: January 16, 2023]

[18] USEtox. Official USEtox 2.13 model and factors [Internet]. 2023. Available from: https://usetox.org/ [Accessed: January 16, 2023]

[19] Dumont M. Assessing biodiversity impacts with BioScope [Internet]. 2022. Available from: https://pre-sustainability.com/articles/assessing-biodiversity-impacts-bioscope/ [Accessed: January 16, 2023]

[20] Bach R, Mohtashami N, Hildebrand L. Comparative overview on LCA software programs for application in the façade design process. Journal of Facade Design & Engineering. 2019;7:1. DOI: 10.7480/jfde.2019.1.2657

[21] Bach R, Hildebrand L. A comparative overview of tools for environmental assessment of materials, components and buildings. In: Kosanovic S, Klein T, Konstaniou T, Fikfak A, Hildebrand L, editors. Sustainable and Resilient Building Design – Approaches, Methods and Tools. Holland: TU Delft Open; 2018. pp. 143-158. ISBN: 978-94-6366-032-7

[22] Silva D, Nunes AO, da Silva MA, Moro C, Piekarski TOR. How important is the LCA software tool you choose? Comparative results from GaBi, openLCA, SimaPro and Umberto, Conference Paper. In: Proceedings of the VII Conferencia Internacional de Análisis de Ciclo de Vida en Latinoamérica, Medellin, Colombia. 2017:10-15

[23] European Commission. European platform on life cycle assessment [Internet]. Available from: https://eplca.jrc.ec.europa.eu/ResourceDirectory/faces/tools/toolList.xhtml [Accessed: January 16, 2023]

[24] Sphera. Life cycle assessment product sustainability (GaBi) [Internet]. 2023. Available from: https://sphera.com/life-cycle-assessment-lca-software/ [Accessed: January 16, 2023]

[25]] SimaPro, PRé Sustainability B.V. LCA software for informed change-makers [Internet]. 2023. Available from: https://simapro.com/ [Accessed: January 16, 2023]

[26] Umberto. LCA software for life cycle assessment [Internet]. 2023. Available from: https://www.ifu.com/umberto/lca-software/ [Accessed: January 16, 2023]

[27] Openlca. The world's leading, high performance, Open Source Life Cycle Assessment Software [Internet]. 2022. Available from: https://www.openlca.org/ [Accessed: January 16, 2023]

[28] Herrmann IT, Moltesen A. Does it matter which life cycle assessment (LCA) tool you choose? A comparative assessment of SimaPro and GaBi. Journal of Cleaner Production. 2015;**86**:163-169. DOI: 10.1016/j.jclepro.2014.08.004

[29] Levi Strauss & CO. [Internet]. 2015. The life cycle of a jean: Understanding the environmental impact of a pair of Levi's 501 jeans, Available from: https://www.levistrauss.com/wp-content/uploads/2015/03/Full-LCA-Results-Deck-FINAL.pdf [Accessed: January 20, 2023]

[30] Hackett T. A comparative life cycle assessment of denim jeans and a cotton t-shirt: The Production of fast fashion essential items from cradle to gate [Dissertation], University of Kentucky, USA, 2015

[31] Karthik T, Murugan R. Chapter 6 – Carbon footprint in denim manufacturing. In: Muthu SS, editor. Sustainability in Denim, Textile Institute Book Series. Cambridge, UK: Woodhead Publishing; 2017:125-159

[32] Vos RO. The spatially explicit water footprint of blue jeans: Spatial methods in action for sustainable consumer products and corporate management of water. Case Studies in the Environment. 2019;**3**(1):1-14

[33] Morita AM, Moore CCS, Nogueira AR, Kulay L, Ravagnani MADSS. Assessment of potential alternatives for improving environmental trouser jeans manufacturing performance in Brazil. Journal of Cleaner Production. 2020;**247**:119156

[34] Akı SU, Candan C, Nergis B, Önder NS. Understanding denim recycling: A quantitative study with lifecycle assessment methodology. In: Körlü A, editor. Waste in Textile and Leather Sectors. London, UK, Rijeka: IntechOpen; 2020

[35] Akı SU, Candan C, Nergis B, Önder NS. An evaluation of recycled polymeric materials usage in denim with lifecycle assessment methodology. In: Achilias DS, editor. Waste Material Recycling in the Circular Economy – Challenges and Developments. London, UK, Rijeka: IntechOpen; 2021

[36] Zhao MY, Zhou Y, Meng J, Zheng HR, Cai YP, Shan YL, et al. Virtual carbon and water flows embodied in global fashion trade – a case study of denim products. Journal of Cleaner Production. 2021;**303**:127080

[37] Fidan FŞ, Aydoğan EK, Uzal N. An integrated life cycle assessment approach for denim fabric production using recycled cotton fibers and combined heat and power plant. Journal of Cleaner Production. 2021;**287**:125439

[38] Fidan FŞ, Aydoğan EK, Uzal N. The impact of organic cotton use and consumer habits in the sustainability of jean production using the LCA approach. Environmental Science and Pollution Research. 2023;**30**:8853-8867. DOI: 10.1007/s11356-022-22872-6

[39] Li X, Ren J, Wu ZS, Wu XY, Ding XM. Development of a novel process-level water footprint assessment for textile production based on modularity. Journal of Cleaner Production. 2021;**291**:125884

[40] Luo Y, Wu X, Ding X. Carbon and water footprints assessment of cotton jeans using the method based on modularity: A full life cycle perspective.

Journal of Cleaner Production. 2022;**332**:130042. DOI: 10.1016/j.jclepro.2021.130042

[41] International Organization for Standardization. Environmental labels and declarations – Type III environmental declarations – principles and procedures (ISO Standard No. 14025:2006). 2006. Retrieved from https://www.iso.org/standard/38131.html

[42] The International EPD® System. Environmental Product Declarations [Internet]. 2023. Available from: https://www.environdec.com/all-about-epds/the-epd [Accessed: February 2, 2023]

[43] The International EPD® System. PCR 2022:04 Fabrics (1.0.1) [Internet]. Available from: https://www.environdec.com/pcr-library [Accessed: February 2, 2023]

[44] SimaPro Database Manual – Methods Library. 2022. Database & support team at PRé sustainability. Available at: https://simapro.com/wp-content/uploads/2022/07/DatabaseManualMethods.pdf

[45] IPCC. GWP 100a: Methodology developed by the Intergovernmental Panel on Climate Change [Internet]. 2013. Available from: http://www.ipcc.ch/ [Accessed: January 1, 2023]

[46] ReCiPe 2016 v1.1. A harmonized life cycle impact assessment method at midpoint and endpoint level Report I: Characterization. RIVM Report 2016-0104a [Internet]. 2017. Available from: http://www.rivm.nl/en/Topics/L/Life_Cycle_Assessment_LCA/Downloads/Documents_ReCiPe2017/Report_ReCiPe_Update_2017 [Accessed: January 1, 2023]

[47] Huijbregts MAJ, Steinmann ZJN, Elshout PMF, Stam G, Verones F, Vieira M, et al. ReCiPe2016: A harmonised life cycle impact assessment method at midpoint and endpoint level. International Journal of Life Cycle Assessment. 2017;**22**:138-147. DOI: 10.1007/s11367-016-1246-y

[48] Guinée JB, Gorrée M, Heijungs R, Huppes G, Kleijn R, Koning A de, et al. Handbook on Life Cycle Assessment. Operational Guide to the ISO Standards. Part III: Scientific Background. Dordrecht: Kluwer Academic Publishers; 2002. p. 692. ISBN: 1-4020-0228-9

[49] Huijbregts MAJ, Breedveld L, Huppes G, De Koning A, Van Oers L, Suh S. Normalisation figures for environmental lifecycle assessment: The Netherlands (1997/1998), Western Europe (1995) and the World (1990 and 1995). Journal of Cleaner Production. 2003;**11**(7):737-748

[50] The International EPD® System – Environmental performance indicators [Internet]. Available from: https://www.environdec.com/indicators [Accessed: February 2, 2023]

Chapter 5

Pathway toward Sustainable Winter Road Maintenance (Case Study)

Katja Malovrh Rebec and Janez Turk

Abstract

Life Cycle Assessment (LCA) method was applied to evaluate the environmental impacts of winter road maintenance managed by an innovative road-weather information system and the impacts of vehicles passing the road during the snowstorm event. A case study refers to 10-hour lasting snowstorm event, considering a specific road section and application of a road-weather information management system to help winter road maintenance agency optimizing activities (salt gritting and/or plowing). Reliable information on the timing of the beginning of the snowstorm event affects (1) the activities of winter road maintenance, (2) the mobility of all vehicles passing the road, and (3) the fuel consumption of the vehicles. Since activities are optimized in case of preventive operation of winter road maintenance, less salt is needed overall. The road remains free of snow cover in case of preventive winter road maintenance operation, meaning that passenger cars and trucks pass the road at normal speed, without undesirable acceleration and braking caused by wheels slipping if snow accumulates on the road. Fuel consumption of vehicles passing salted and snow-free road remains unchanged, while fuel consumption increases in case of snow cover. Reduction of environmental burdens in case of such optimized winter road maintenance operation, is shown in this case study. The overall results of the comparative LCA analysis showed that the use of the road-weather information system in road traffic allows for as much as 25% reduction of environmental footprints. In the scenario where the winter service does not use information system the winter service also uses 40% more salt, which is also related with additional environmental impacts.

Keywords: LCA, environmental impacts, road, snow cover, preventive operation, traffic, fuel consumption, safety

1. Introduction

The transportation sector is one of the key contributors to greenhouse gas emissions that are potentially affecting global warming. A great majority of emissions caused by the transportation sector originate from passenger vehicles and trucks, due to exhaust fumes. The combustion of fossil fuels in engines is thus one of the most important contributors to atmospheric greenhouse gases. Traffic delays, radiative forcing, and rolling resistance are factors, which have a significant impact on the fuel consumption of vehicles and trucks. However, also the management of road infrastructure is directly related with environmental impacts, due to raw material consumption and energy needs during the construction and maintenance of the road, as well as during end-of-life activities [1–3].

European Green Deal introduced several proposals for reducing net greenhouse gas emissions by at least 55% by 2030, compared to the 1990 level. One of the proposals refers to providing efficient, safe, and environmentally sustainable transport [4]. Within this frame, winter road maintenance (WRM) plays an important role. The main activity of WRM agencies is reducing ice and snow from roadways, which is of crucial importance to provide safe driving conditions for traffic and smooth mobility. In countries with cold and humid winters, snowstorms may cause problems in the mobility of road traffic resulting in congestions and delays. In such conditions, fuel economy of vehicles is deteriorated, and consequently emissions increase. From this point of view, ensuring snow- and ice-free road is of great importance to achieve targets set by European Green Deal. However, winter road maintenance also yields a significant amount of greenhouse gases and other emissions, especially in cold regions, with a relatively high frequency of such activities [5]. Moreover, salt and other deicers, which are gritted on the road, pose a negative impact on groundwater and freshwater quality, and consequently also on biodiversity and human health [5, 6]. This represents a serious environmental problem taking into account that significant amounts of road salt and other chemicals are used to remove ice and snow accumulated on the road or to prevent icing and snow compaction on the roads [5]. WRM agencies are under pressure to improve not only the effectiveness and efficiency of their activities but also to optimize the activities from the aspect of sustainability. To improve environmental sustainability, special attention regarding the application of materials, strategies, and equipment is required [7]. Application of best practices from other studies can be a pathway toward achieving environmental sustainability in the field of winter road maintenance.

Several authors addressed the problem of environmental sustainability of winter road maintenance and the number of such studies is growing in recent years. Cui et al. [7] provided a framework for assessing sustainability in the field of winter road maintenance with salt as a road deicer. Adequate selection of deicers (road salt, agro-based, and complex chlorides/minerals-based products) is of crucial importance for successful implementation of winter road maintenance. Decision on selection of deicers has been typically taken based on their cost and effectiveness. However, the environmental impacts of salt or other chemicals used for deicing should also represent an important aspect when deciding about different deicing alternatives. Environmental impacts can be direct, due to release of chemicals into natural environment (soil, surface water), or indirect. The latter refers to the repair of damage (mostly related with corrosion) that deicers cause on vehicles and road infrastructure. Repair of such damage is associated with environmental impacts as well [7].

Environmental impacts related with winter road maintenance in Norway were evaluated in a study by Vignisdottir et al. [5]. They took into account the production and transportation of road salt (deicer) and vehicles for winter road maintenance and the operation of the winter road maintenance (use of the vehicles for plowing and salt spreading, associated with fuel and salt consumption). Data on quantities of road salt used for deicing and data on fuel consumption of WRM vehicles were gathered from public reports, so the results of LCA reflect realistic conditions. The study showed that emissions related to winter road maintenance in Norway contribute around 1% of the total emissions from road transportation in Norway. Such relatively high contribution can be explained by two facts. The first one is that Norway is the leading country in the use of electric and hybrid electric vehicles, which cause zero- and low emissions. The second fact is that most part of Norway has a cold and relatively humid climate. In such regions, winter road maintenance is extensive.

Vignisdottir et al. [8] provided a comprehensive review of 35 scientific papers dedicated to the evaluation of environmental impacts and effects of winter road maintenance. Based on this review, some research gaps were emphasized. In most of studies, only local environmental effects of deicers were addressed. While rare studies provide a holistic overview on environmental impacts related with winter road maintenance operation methods or material selection.

The goal of this study is to compare the environmental impacts of two scenarios related to the operation of winter road maintenance. Life Cycle Assessment (LCA) method was applied to conduct such a comparison. In baseline scenario, the agency responsible for WRM does not use a road-weather information system, meaning that it does not have accurate information about the exact timing of the beginning of the snowstorm event. Winter road maintenance operations start only when snow began accumulating on the road.

In alternative scenario, the WRM agency does use road-weather information system. In such a case, it obtains reliable information on timing of snowfall event and if snow or ice will accumulate on the road. Based on such detailed weather forecast, the WRM agency can take preventive measures, and if necessary, start gritting the road just before the snowfall event. In such conditions, the agency can optimize the consumption of road salt required for anti-icing and/or deicing. The purpose of this study is to benchmark the environmental impacts of baseline WRM operation scenario versus alternative scenario (preventive WRM operation scenario).

2. Materials and methods

Typical winter road maintenance activity is the mechanical removal of snow accompanied by deicing with chemicals or traction enhancement with abrasives. To conduct such activities, vehicles equipped with liquid and solid spreaders, and plows are required. Plowing and/or spreading of deicer are associated with the consumption of fuel (vehicles are typically run on diesel) and deicers, which are most commonly salt and sand [6, 9]. Other deicers can also be used, such as calcium chloride, magnesium chloride, agro-based products, acetates, formates, glycols, and succinates [9].

Special Road-Weather Information Systems (RWIS) have been designed for WRM agencies to help them evaluating road conditions in cold climates in a way, that they can optimize the timing of salting and plowing activities [10]. By using Road-Weather Information System, the WRM agency obtains reliable information about the timing of snowfall on a particular section of the road and about the bonding of the snow with the road surface. The system is based on physical, energy-balance model to predict road conditions such as dry, wet, snowy, icy, for every hour and for 12 hours in advance. The forecast is high-resolution in time (forecast per every hour) and space (forecast for every km of road section).

2.1 Scenarios

2.1.1 Baseline WRM operation scenario

WRM agency does not use Road-Weather Information System and for this reason, the activities related with road maintenance (gritting with salt and plowing) begin only when the snow is already bonding with the road surface. During a long-lasting snowstorm, the WRM vehicle must pass the road section several times. The vehicle conducts gritting and plowing simultaneously. Fuel consumption of the WRM vehicle is increased because the vehicle drives in demanding weather conditions (when the snow is already bonding with the road surface). Moreover, the use of a plow has a direct impact on the relatively higher fuel consumption of the WRM vehicle. Other vehicles (passenger cars, trucks) passing the road section during snowstorms must adapt their driving to the snow conditions on the road. Fuel consumption of vehicles driving on the road is higher, which means that associated emissions are also higher. In general, snow and ice coverage on a road surface increase the fuel consumption of vehicles. The wheels can slip on the road, wasting energy as they have reduced grip, while driving speeds are significantly lower than normal [11]. For the purpose of this study, it was assumed that the corresponding increase in fuel consumption is 10, 20, and 30% respectively. This assumption is supported by literature data [12–14].

2.1.2 Preventive WRM operation scenario

Taking into account information obtained by Road-Weather Information System, the WRM agency can perform a preventive operation and start gritting with salt just before the beginning of the snowfall and its bonding with the road surface. The effectiveness of preventive activity (e.g., gritting with salt or some other anti-icing agent) is strongly linked to precise timing of the activity. The WRM vehicle conducts the preventive gritting with an anti-icing agent (salt) still on a dry road, while subsequent gritting operations are conducted during snowfall, on a wet, but still snow and ice-free road (meaning that plowing is not needed). The number of subsequent operations depends on the duration of weather event (e.g., snowstorm). The first preventive and subsequent gritting operations result in snow melting, so there is no snow accumulation on the road surface. In such conditions, the WRM agency uses up to 40% less salt than in baseline WRM operation scenario. Other vehicles passing the road section during the snowstorm event may drive at normal speeds, adapted to conditions of the wet road surface. Vehicles do not consume more fuel than usual. If so, emissions related to exhaust gases do not increase compared to normal weather conditions.

2.2 Life cycle assessment

The environmental impacts in the two scenarios were assessed using the Life Cycle Assessment (LCA) method. LCA is a standardized (SIST EN ISO 14040:2006) and internationally recognized method for assessing the potential environmental impacts of the products or processes under study. The LCA method is often used to evaluate the environmental impacts of comparable technologies or processes. In this study, LCA was applied to compare the environmental performance of two scenarios related to the operation of winter road maintenance. The optimized operation was evaluated against the classical operation of the WRM vehicle during a particular snowstorm event. Holistic environmental benchmarking of two scenarios, which take into account also mobility of all road vehicles passing the road during the weather event, was the main goal of this LCA study.

The functional unit of the LCA is the operation of WRM vehicles due to a particular snowstorm event. The weather event lasted 10 hours and the snow cover reached a thickness of 25 cm. Alternatively, the functional unit can take into account also mobility of all road vehicles passing the road section during the weather event. The length of the road section is 10.4 km. The functional unit thus includes the use the WRM vehicle (fuel consumption and related emissions) which conducts gritting (consumption of road salt) and when necessary the simultaneous plowing (the latter in case the baseline WRM operation scenario, when snow is assumed to accumulate on the road surface), as well as road traffic passing the road section during the weather event (fuel consumption and related emissions). Mobility of passenger vehicles and trucks, or disturbance in their mobility, has a direct impact on emissions to the environment.

2.3 System boundaries and assumptions

The system boundaries for the baseline WRM operation scenario where the WRM agency does not use Road-Weather Information System are shown in **Figure 1**. The WRM vehicle has to pass the road section four times during a snowstorm event. The length of the road section is 10.4 km; therefore the vehicle travels 41.6 km. The WRM vehicle conducts gritting and plowing simultaneously. The salt consumption is 40% higher than in the preventive WRM operation scenario, reaching 10 tons (**Table 1**). Because of the plowing, the fuel consumption of the WRM vehicle increases to around 50 L per 100 km (**Table 1**). Other vehicles passing the road section during snowstorm event must adapt their driving to the snow conditions on the road. We assumed fuel consumption to be 10 or even 20% higher in

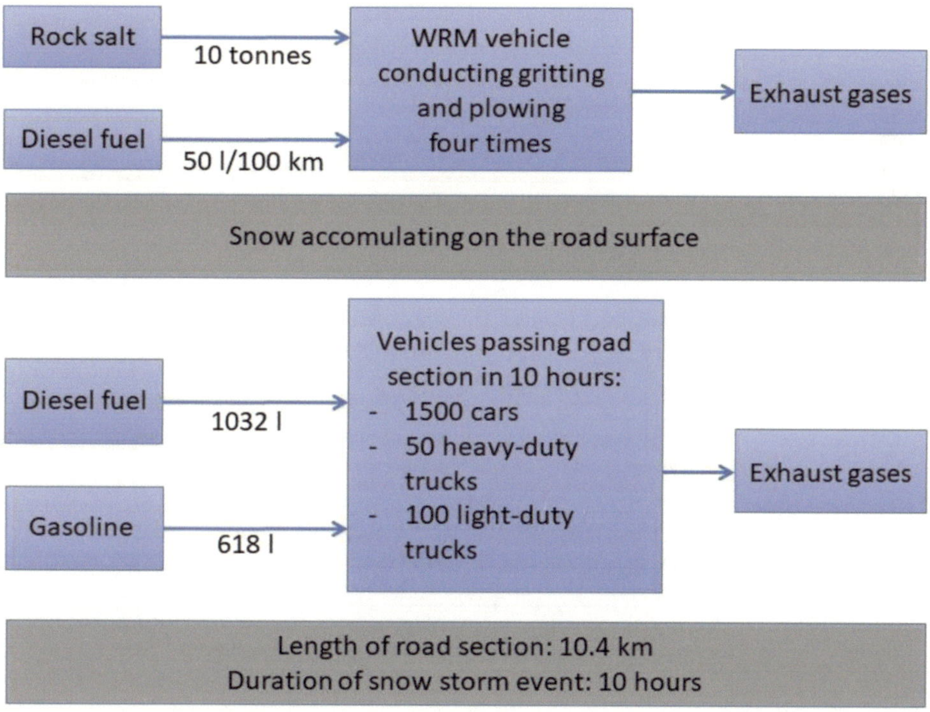

Figure 1.
System boundaries for the baseline WRM operation scenario.

case of driving on a road with snow bonding compared to driving on snow-free road (**Table 1**).

The system boundaries for the preventive WRM operation scenario, where the WRM agency uses Road-Weather Information System are shown in **Figure 2**. In this scenario, the WRM vehicle drives at normal speed (30 km/h), consuming around 40 L of diesel fuel per 100 km (**Table 2**). The WRM vehicle conducts a preventive gritting before the beginning of the snowfall and two more gritting operations during the snowfall event lasting for 10 hours. The 6 tons of road salt are required for such an operation, taking into account the length of the road section (10.4 km) and the fact that the WRM vehicle passes the road section three times. No plowing is required. All other vehicles passing the road section during a snowstorm event are assumed to be able to drive at normal speed. The fuel consumption of vehicles was accounted accordingly (see **Table 2**).

The data on the number of vehicles passing the particular road section considered in this study are from the year 2020. Data were obtained from the two traffic counting points located along the road section. It was assumed that the daily traffic in the

Equipment, material/energy requirements	Data inventory	Process description	Amount
Winter road maintenance vehicle	GLO: Truck, Euro 5, 12–14 t gross weight /9.3 t payload capacity	1 vehicle conducting salt gritting and snow plowing—passing the road Section 4 times	Diesel fuel consumption 50 L/100 km
Road salt	EU-28: Sodium chloride (rock salt)	Road salt gritting	10.000 kg
Heavy-duty trucks	GLO: Truck, Euro 5, 28–32 t gross weight / 22 t payload capacity	50 trucks passing the road section	Diesel fuel consumption 41 L/100 km or 44.7 L/100 km
Light-duty trucks	GLO: Truck, Euro 5, 7.5 t–12 t gross weight / 5 t payload capacity	100 trucks passing the road section	Diesel fuel consumption 25.5 L/100 km or 27.8 L/100 km
Diesel passenger cars	GLO: Car, diesel, Euro 5, engine size 1.4-2 l	600 diesel passenger cars passing the road section	Diesel fuel consumption 5.5 L/100 km or 6 L/100 km
Petrol passenger cars	GLO: Car, petrol, Euro 5, engine size 1.4-2 l	900 petrol passenger cars passing the road section	Gasoline consumption 6.6 L/100 km or 7.2 L/100 km
Diesel fuel	EU-28: Diesel mix at filling station	Diesel fuel for trucks and passenger cars passing the road section	1032 L
Gasoline (petrol)	EU-28: Gasoline mix (regular) at filling station	Petrol fuel for passenger cars passing the road section	618 L

Table 1.
Input data for baseline WRM operation scenario without application of road-weather information system. Winter road maintenance operation and road traffic mobility during snowstorm events are adapted to conditions with snow accumulating on the road surface.

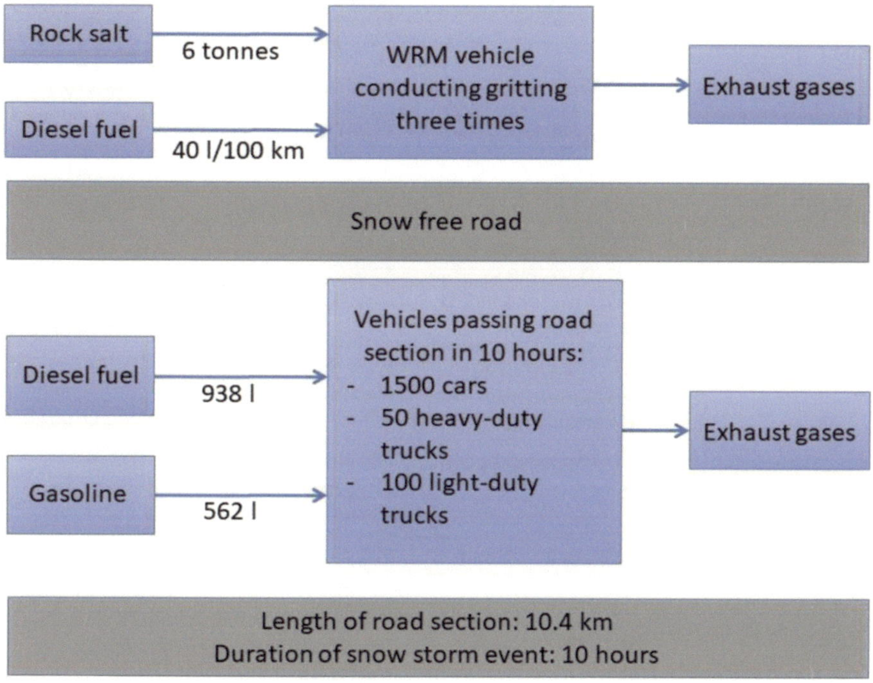

Figure 2.
System boundaries for the preventive WRM operation scenario.

studied section is the average number from the two counting points. Based on these data, it was assumed that during a 10-hour weather event, the road section is passed by 1500 passenger cars, 100 light-duty trucks, and 50 heavy-duty trucks. For passenger cars, we assumed that 40% of them are diesel cars and 60% are petrol cars, which is realistic information for Slovenian conditions, to which the case study refers.

2.4 Life cycle inventory analysis

GaBi professional software (version 10.6) was used to conduct a comparative LCA analysis. Data related with the use stage of vehicles, data for the production of fuels required for vehicles and data for deicer were gathered from the Professional database, which is integrated into GaBi software. Inventory data applied in two scenarios are indicated in **Table 1** (baseline WRM operation scenario without application of Road-Weather Information System) and **Table 2** (preventive WRM operation scenario with the application of Road-Weather Information System).

2.5 Impact assessment

ReCiPe 2016 version 1.1 Life Cycle Assessment Impact method was used to evaluate the environmental impacts of two scenarios. The ReCiPe method was developed in 2008 to harmonize the results of two other methods, CML 2001 (midpoint-oriented) and Eco-indicator 99 (endpoint-oriented). ReCiPe is one of the most commonly used methods for the calculation of environmental impacts [15]. The main principles of the ReCiPe 2016 method are based on the ISO 14040 and 14044 standards. The characterization factors are continuously updated according

Equipment, material/ energy requirements	Data inventory	Process description	Amount
Winter road maintenance vehicle	GLO: Truck, Euro 5, 12—14 t gross weight/9.3 t payload capacity	1 vehicle conducting salt gritting—passing the road Section 3 times	Diesel fuel consumption 40 L/100 km
Road salt	EU-28: Sodium chloride (rock salt)	Road salt gritting	6000 kg
Heavy-duty trucks	GLO: Truck, Euro 5, 28–32 t gross weight/22 t payload capacity	50 trucks passing the road section	Diesel fuel consumption 37.3 L/100 km
Light-duty trucks	GLO: Truck, Euro 5, 7.5–12 t gross weight / 5 t payload capacity	100 trucks passing the road section	Diesel fuel consumption 23.2 L/100 km
Diesel passenger cars	GLO: Car, diesel, Euro 5, engine size 1.4-2 l	600 diesel passenger cars passing the road section	Diesel fuel consumption 5 L/100 km
Petrol passenger cars	GLO: Car, petrol, Euro 5, engine size 1.4-2 l	900 petrol passenger cars passing the road section	Gasoline consumption 6 L/100 km
Diesel fuel	EU-28: Diesel mix at filling station	Diesel fuel for trucks and passenger cars passing the road section	938 L
Gasoline (petrol)	EU-28: Gasoline mix (regular) at filling station	Petrol fuel for passenger cars passing the road section	562 L

Table 2.
Input data for preventive WRM operation scenario: Winter road maintenance operation and road traffic mobility in case of application of road-weather information system take place on road, which is snow- and ice-free.

to new knowledge [16, 17]. The ReCiPe 2016 method allows the calculation of impact categories according to three-time perspectives (Individualist, Hierarchist, and Egalitarian). The Hierarchist perspective, which considers the most acceptable time period, is used in this study. The LCA results at the midpoint levels are presented by 19 impact categories (**Table 3**).

3. Results and discussion

First, only environmental impacts associated with the operation of WRM vehicles in two alternative scenarios were evaluated. The results show that the production of road salt (rock salt respectively) required for gritting the road yields significantly higher environmental impacts than the operation of the WRM vehicle itself. Production of road salt contributes 90% or more to the total parameter value of all impacts categories, the only exception is the impact on ozone layer depletion potential, where salt contributes around 70% of the total parameter value. Operation of the WRM vehicle is associated with diesel fuel requirements and exhaust gas emissions due to fuel combustion. These kinds of environmental impacts are thus relatively minor compared to impacts associated with salt gritting. Those are even

Impact category	Abbreviation	Unit
Climate change, default, excl. Biogenic carbon	GWP_default	kg CO_2 eq.
Climate change, incl. Biogenic carbon	GWP_incl. biog. C	kg CO_2 eq.
Fine Particulate Matter Formation	PM 2.5	kg PM2.5 eq
Fossil depletion	ADP_f	kg oil eq.
Freshwater Consumption	FWC	m^3
Freshwater ecotoxicity	FWAETP	kg 1,4 DB eq.
Freshwater Eutrophication	FWEP	kg P eq.
Human toxicity, cancer	HTP_cancer	kg 1,4-DB eq.
Human toxicity, non-cancer	HTP_non_cancer	kg 1,4-DB eq.
Ionizing Radiation	IR	kBq Co-60 eq. to air
Land use	LU	Annual crop eq.·y
Marine ecotoxicity	MWAETP	kg 1,4-DB eq.
Marine Eutrophication	MWEP	kg N eq.
Metal depletion	MD	Kg Cu eq.
Photochemical Ozone Formation, Ecosystems	POCP_ecosystem	kg NOx eq.
Photochemical Ozone Formation, Human Health	POCP_human_health	kg NOx eq.
Stratospheric Ozone Depletion	ODP	kg CFC-11 eq.
Terrestrial Acidification	AP	kg SO_2 eq.
Terrestrial ecotoxicity	TETP	kg 1,4-DB eq.

Table 3.
ReCiPe 2016 midpoint impact categories.

underestimated in this LCA study, as impacts of salt flushed into water or terrestrial ecosystems are not possible to evaluate by means of LCA. The fate of road salt released in the environment is poorly understood and because of this reason, no characterization factors for leaching of salt into the natural environment have been introduced in LCA [5, 7, 9].

A comparison of two scenarios shows that the use of the Road-Weather Information System can significantly contribute to a reduction of environmental impacts related to the operation of winter road maintenance. This is a direct consequence of optimization in the consumption of salt for gritting the road. In this specific case study, the WRM agency reported that they saved 40% of road salt due to preventive winter road maintenance operations. Environmental impacts were reduced between 43% (in case of photochemical ozone creation potential—POCP) and 36% (in case of ozone layer depletion potential—ODP) compared to the baseline WRM operation scenario. In most of the impact categories, the impacts were reduced by 39% (including in the case of global warming potential—GWP, abiotic depletion of fossil fuels—ADP-f, and human toxicity potential—HTP). Optimization of the operation of winter road maintenance in terms of less operational activities of the vehicle (e.g., less fuel consumption due to a lower number of travels along road section and conducting only gritting, no plowing) yields relatively minor contribution to environmental improvement of preventive WRM operation scenario compared to baseline WRM operation scenario (**Figure 3**).

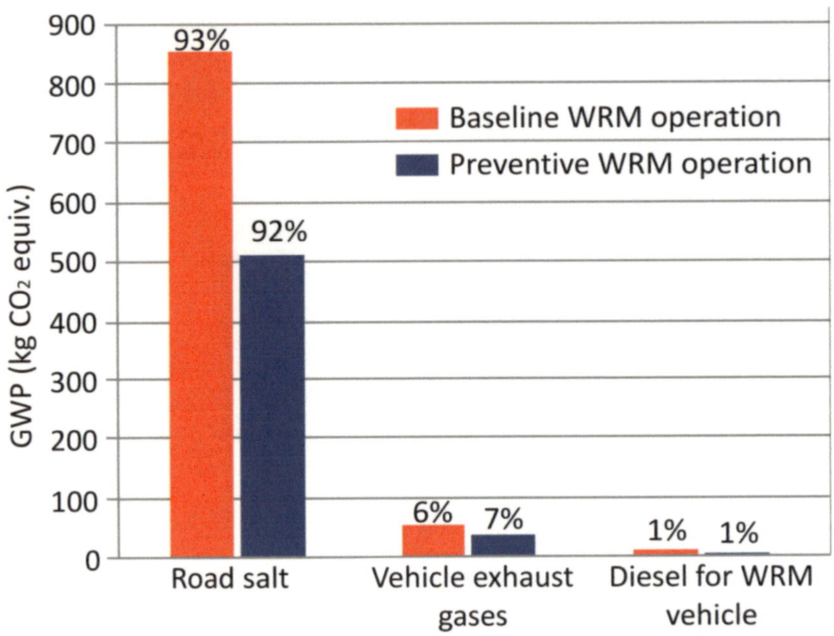

Figure 3.
Global warming potential associated with the operation of WRM vehicle (salt gritting, fuel consumption, and related exhaust gases) in two benchmarked scenarios.

In addition, two scenarios were compared by means of LCA holistically, accounting also environmental impacts caused by road traffic (passenger cars and trucks) passing the road section during a weather event. In such a case, the LCA results are greatly influenced by density of road traffic. Denser the traffic is, the higher is its contribution to the environmental impact of the studied system. It was assumed that road traffic in demanding winter conditions (due to snow accumulation on the road) consumes 10% of fuel more than in normal driving conditions (snow-free road). In case of baseline scenario, the traffic contributes around 80–90% of the total parameter values, depending on the impact category (the contribution is 84% in case of global warming potential—**Figure 4**). The rest of the influence is mostly affected by road salt, while the contribution of WRM vehicles is reasonably minor as already discussed. In a scenario with preventive WRM operation, environmental loads are reduced typically by 14% (GWP for example) compared to the baseline scenario. However, the impact on ionizing radiation is reduced even by 31%, due to less salt (anti-icing agent) consumption (**Figure 5**). Mining of rock salt is associated with electricity requirements. Taking into account that an important share of European electricity derives from nuclear power plants, such electricity yields a relatively high ionizing radiation footprint. This footprint is accounted also to resources (e.g., rock salt) for which exploitation requires electrical power. Moreover, an important share of electricity derives from thermal power plants. For this reason, mining of rock salt yields also relatively high impacts on fine particulate matter formation (PM 2.5), photochemical ozone formation (POCP), and acidification potential (AP). Because of less consumption of salt in preventive WRM operation scenarios, impacts on these three impact categories are also quite significantly reduced (PM 2.5 for 19%, POCP for 18%, and AP for 17%) (**Figure 5**).

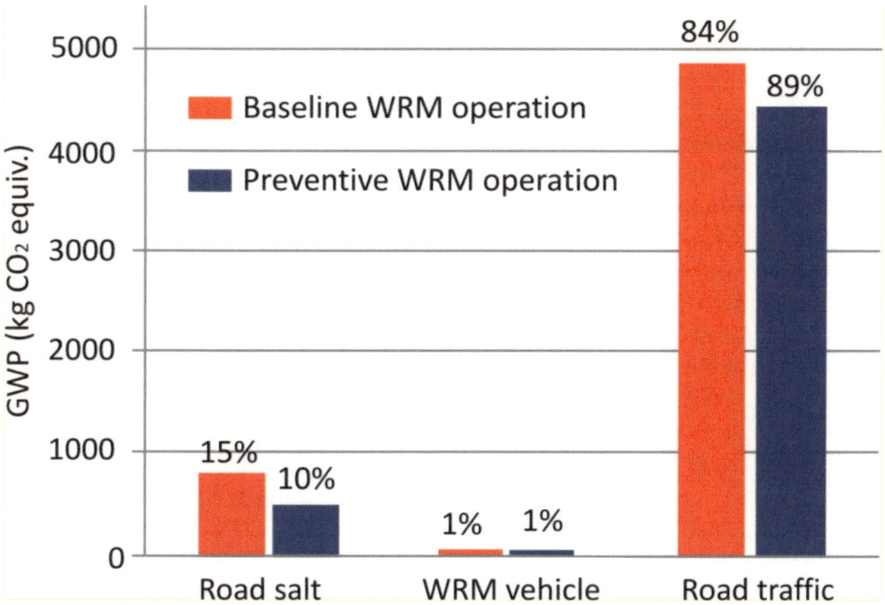

Figure 4.
Global warming potential of baseline WRM operation scenario versus preventive WRM operation scenario. Contributions of road salt, WRM vehicle (fuel consumption and associated exhaust emissions), and road traffic (fuel consumption and associated exhaust emissions) to GWP are shown in absolute and relative values.

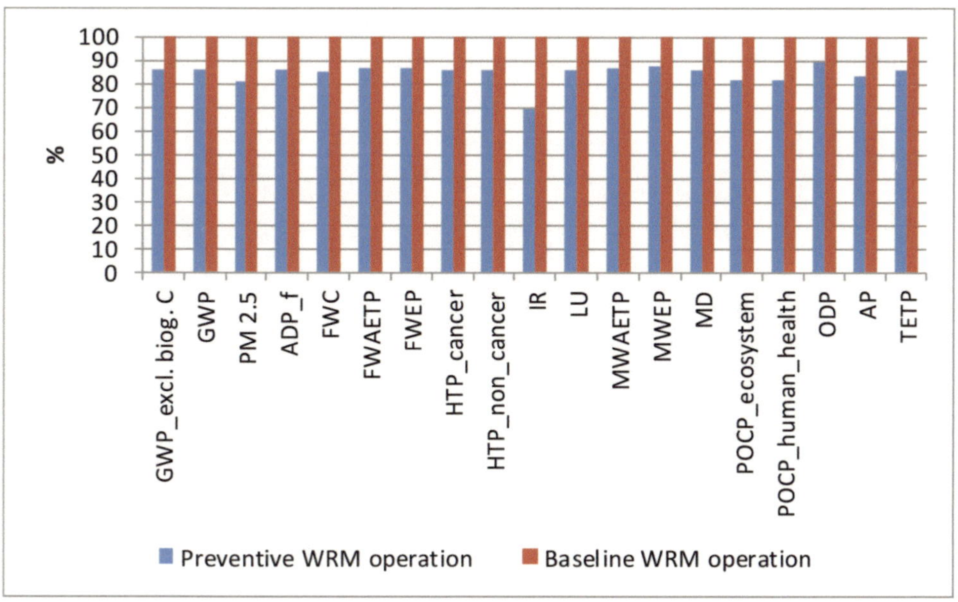

Figure 5.
Relative comparison of two scenarios. Baseline WRM operation scenario is set as a reference.

3.1 Uncertainty analysis

Uncertainty refers to data on fuel consumption of passenger cars and trucks passing the road section during a snowstorm event. Literature data indicate that increases in fuel consumption in different levels of slush vary between 10 and 30% [12–14]. Indeed, the practical experiences of the authors of this study showed that fuel consumption of passenger cars driving on roads with 10 cm snow cover increases by nearly 30%. In general, it was assumed that passenger cars and trucks consume 10% more fuel when driving on a road with snow cover, compared to driving on snow-free roads. If we assume that the traffic driving on the road with snow cover consumes 20% of fuel more than in normal driving conditions (preventive WRM operation scenario), then such a baseline scenario shows even greater environmental impacts. In such a case, differences between the two scenarios are typically 20% (GWP for example) or even more for some impact categories (up to 33% in case of impact on ionizing radiation). If we assume that the road traffic in the baseline WRM operation scenario consumes even 30% of fuel more than in preventive WRM operation scenario, the differences between the two scenarios are typically 25% (in terms of GWP, abiotic depletion of fossil fuels, human toxicity, ecotoxicity indicators etc.) and maximally 34% (in terms of ionizing radiation—IR) (**Figure 6**).

However, totally opposed findings can also be found in the literature regarding the fuel consumption of vehicles traveling on the road with snow cover. Taking into account the study of Nordin and Arvidsson [18], the fuel consumption of vehicles does not increase in conditions with 1 cm of snow cover on a road. Argumentation is that demanding driving conditions related with slippery roads or reduced visibility forces drivers to reduce the speed. Lower speed of vehicles due to the presence of small amounts of snow can result even in lower fuel consumption compared to vehicles on a cleared road driving with the usual speed [18]. But this is certainly not the case when snow cover on road reaches a few centimeters [12–14].

However, opposing findings can also be found in the literature regarding the fuel consumption of vehicles traveling on the road with snow cover. Taking into account

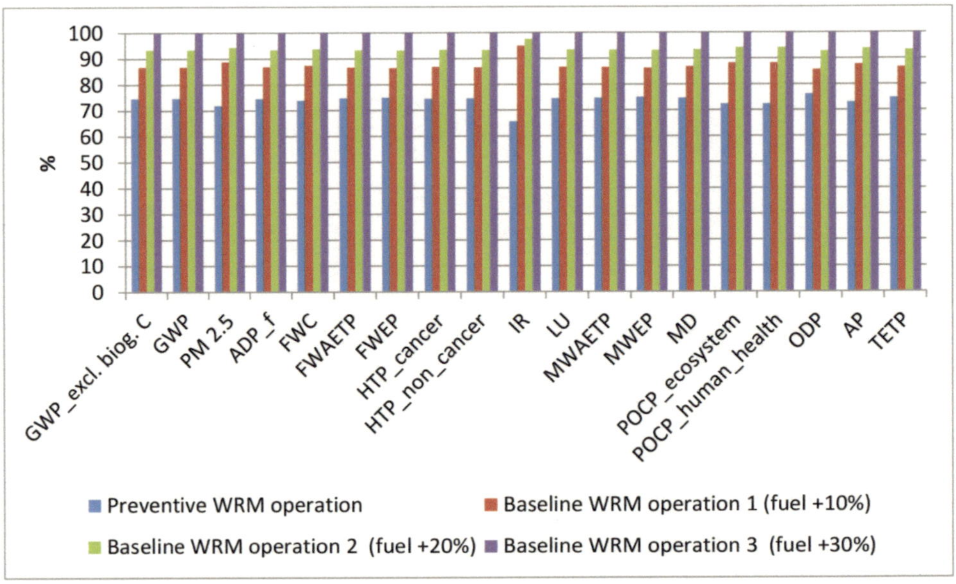

Figure 6.
Relative comparison of baseline WRM operation scenario versus preventive WRM operation scenario. In case of baseline WRM operation scenario, three assumptions were taken into account regarding the fuel consumption of cars and trucks passing the road covered with snow: 10, 20, or 30% increase in fuel consumption due to the presence of snow on the road. The assumption with the highest fuel consumption was set as a reference.

the study of Nordin and Arvidsson [18], the fuel consumption of vehicles does not increase in conditions with 1 cm of snow cover on a road. Argumentation is that demanding driving conditions related with slippery road or reduced visibility force drivers to reduce the speed. Lower speed of vehicles due to the presence of small amounts of snow can result even in lower fuel consumption compared to vehicles on a cleared road driving with the usual speed [18].

4. Conclusions

The importance of optimizing winter road maintenance operations for achieving goals of environmental sustainability in the transportation sector is presented in a practical case study. Environmental impacts can be significantly reduced if the agency responsible for winter road maintenance optimizes the timing of operations and in this way uses less salt for road gritting. Moreover, the precise timing of winter road maintenance operations is of crucial importance for enabling smooth and undisturbed mobility of road traffic passing the road during a snowstorm event. Fuel consumption of road traffic and related exhaust emissions increase in case of disturbances and congestion due to snow accumulation on the road.

Currently, vehicles operating on fossil fuels still dominate road traffic in most countries. Ensuring smooth, undisturbed mobility of road traffic during snowstorm events is of great importance from an environmental point of view. For this reason, optimized in-time operation of winter road maintenance in case of snowstorm events can significantly contribute to a reduction of environmental pollution and achieving goals proposed in the European Green Deal for reducing net greenhouse gas emissions. However, it can be assumed that electric vehicles will dominate road traffic in the next decades. But heavy-duty trucks run on diesel fuel will likely be used for a longer period of time. Electric vehicles do not cause exhaust emissions on the road, however, there are indirect emissions taking place at power plants etc. These emissions depend on the share of electricity derived from renewable or non-renewable resources used for charging electric vehicles. Anyway, driving conditions (road with snow cover, snow-free road) may not have a significant impact on indirect emissions caused by road traffic with electric vehicles. But, the importance of providing safe driving conditions, due to optimized in-time operation of winter road maintenance will remain. Optimized road salt consumption will still be of great importance to reduce environmental impacts such as global warming potential, abiotic depletion of mineral resources, human toxicity, and eco-toxicity-related impacts.

Acknowledgements

The research was financially supported by the Slovenian Research Agency (Research Core Funding No. P2-0273). The authors would also like to thank Pomgrad d.d. company and dr. Alenka Šajn Slak from CGS Labs d.o.o. company for providing the data required for this LCA study.

Author details

Katja Malovrh Rebec* and Janez Turk
Slovenian National Building and Civil Engineering Institute, Ljubljana, Slovenia

*Address all correspondence to: katja.malovrh@zag.si

References

[1] Bharadwaj S, Ballare S, Chandel MK. Impact of congestion on greenhouse gas emissions for road transport in Mumbai metropolitan region. Transportation Research Procedia. 2017;**25**:3538-3551. DOI: 10.1016/j.trpro.2017.05.282

[2] Shani P, Chau S, Swei O. All roads lead to sustainability: Opportunities to reduce the life-cycle cost and global warming impact of U.S. roadways. Resources, Conservation and Recycling. 2021;**173**:105701. DOI: 10.1016/j.resconrec.2021.105701

[3] Hoffmann C, Thommes K. Clear roads and dirty air? Indirect effects of reduced private traffic congestion on emissions from heavy traffic. Journal of Cleaner Production. 2022;**381**:135053

[4] European Commission: A European Green Deal. 2019. Available from: https://ec.europa.eu/info/strategy/priorities-2019-2024/european-green-deal_en#actions [Accessed: December 16, 2022]

[5] Vignisdottir HR, Ebrahimi B, Booto GK, et al. Life cycle assessment of winter road maintenance. International Journal of Life Cycle Assessment. 2020;**25**:646-666. DOI: 10.1007/s11367-019-01682-y

[6] Boselly SE. Benefit/Cost Study of RWIS and Anti-icing Technologies. Final report. Prepared for National Cooperative Highway Research Program Transportation Research Board National Research Council. 2001. Available from: https://sicop-dev.transportation.org/wp-content/uploads/sites/36/2017/07/NCHRP-20-07117_B-C-of-RWIS-Antiicing_2001.pdf [Accessed: December 16, 2022]

[7] Cui N, Xie N, Shi X. A Framework for Life-Cycle Sustainability Assessment of Road Salt Used in Winter Maintenance Operations. In: Shi X, Fu L., editors. Sustainable Winter Road Operations. 1st ed. Wiley; 2018. Available from: https://onlinelibrary.wiley.com/doi/pdf/10.1002/9781119185161.fmatter [Accessed: December 16, 2022]

[8] Vignisdottir HR, Booto GK, Bohne RA, Brattebø H, Ebrahimi B, Wallbaum H, et al. A review of environmental impacts of winter road maintenance. Cold Regions Science and Technology. 2019;**158**:143-153. DOI: 10.1016/j.coldregions.2018.10.013

[9] Terry LG, Conaway K, Rebar J, et al. Alternative deicers for winter road maintenance—A review. Water, Air, and Soil Pollution. 2020;**231**:394. DOI: 10.1007/s11270-020-04773-x

[10] Nazari R, Wang H, Chen X, Spanos N, Minner N, Perdomo C, et al. Road Weather Information Systems for Winter Road Maintenance. 2018. DOI: 10.13140/RG.2.2.19934.25922. Available from: https://www.researchgate.net/publication/347727334_Road_Weather_Information_Systems_for_Winter_Road_Maintenance [Accessed: December 16, 2022]

[11] Zacharof N, Fontaras G, Ciuffo B, Tsiakmakis S, et al. Review of in use factors affecting the fuel consumption and CO_2 emissions of passenger cars. JRC Science for Policy Report. EUR 27819 EN. 2016. DOI: 10.2790/140640. Available from: https://op.europa.eu/en/publication-detail/-/publication/bd6b3daa-ad66-11e6-aab7-01aa75ed71a1/language-en [Accessed: December 16, 2022]

[12] Carlson A, Vieira T. The effect of water and snow on the road surface on

rolling resistance. VTI Rapport 971A. 2021

[13] Fontaras G, Zacharof NK, Ciuffo B. Fuel consumption and CO2 emissions from passenger cars in Europe—Laboratory versus real-world emissions. Progress in Energy and Combustion Science. 2017;**60**:97-131

[14] Wallman CG, Wretling P, Öberg G. Effects of Winter Road Maintenance—State of the Art. VTI rapport 423A. 1997

[15] Huijbregts MAJ, Steinmann J, Elshout PMF, Stam G, Verones F, Vieira MDM, et al. ReCiPe2016: A harmonised life cycle impact assessment method at midpoint and endpoint level. International Journal of Life Cycle Assessment. 2017;**22**:138-147. DOI: 10.1007/s11367-016-1246-y

[16] Guinée JB, Gorrée M, Heijungs R, Huppes G, Kleijn R, Koning A, et al. Handbook on life cycle assessment. In: Operational Guide to the ISO Standards. I: LCA in Perspective. IIa: Guide. IIb: Operational Annex. III: Scientific Background. Dordrecht: Kluwer Academic Publishers; 2002. p. 692

[17] Goedkoop M, Heijungs R, Huijbregts M, Schryver AD, Struijs J, Zelm RV. ReCiPe 2008—A Life Cycle Impact Assessment Method Which Comprises Harmonised Category Indicators at the Midpoint and the Endpoint Level. First Edition Report I, Characterisation, VROM, Den Haag. 2008

[18] Nordin L, Arvidsson AK. Are winter road maintenance practices energy efficient? A geographical analysis in terms of traffic energy use. Journal of Transport Geography. 2014;**41**:163-174

Chapter 6

The Life Cycle in Startup Valuation

Sergio Rafael Bravo Orellana

Abstract

The business valuation process begins with the projection of the company's sales or income, so it is important to establish how they will evolve over time. It is possible to verify that the businesses follow a common pattern in the evolution of their income, and these have a trend line in the form of an S inclined forward, defining the life cycle of the business. When new companies (startups) are valued, it is important to visualize their life cycle, since it usually takes time for them to generate profits or positive cash flows, therefore the investment stage and the moment where they prove their viability are prolonged. If these startups correspond to businesses based on the intensive use of technologies, their life cycles show an even greater trend in the duration of the investment stage, the introduction stage is slow, but if they managed to be successful ventures, they have rapid growth and their largest dimensions market, until reaching the stage of maturity. However, not all technological businesses are similar, so for the analysis the type of innovation with which the business worked must be considered, since the shape of the life cycle will be different in the investment period, the speed of growth and the size of the market.

Keywords: financial value equity, life cycle, Startup Valuation, Startups, economic flows

1. Introduction

1.1 The life cycle in business

The valuation of the shareholders' equity is made from the projection of company profits (income minus costs) or cash flows (income minus expenses). The construction of these statements and economic flows means that each of its components must be projected, for which assumptions are made about the evolution of the company's fundamentals (prices, sales volume, costs and expenses). The projections of each variable are not independent, since they are carried out taking as a point of reference the projection of sales or income of the company. Based on this projection, those corresponding to costs and expenses are made, including projections of investments in assets and working capital.

From this process, the importance of the way in which sales evolve is clear; In this sense, it is important to analyze the concept of the business life cycle, since it describes the evolution of sales since the beginning of the company's operations. The first sales with Chart with the product ***introduction stage***; if the company's products reach market acceptance, the ***growth stage begins***; When sales are consolidated in the target

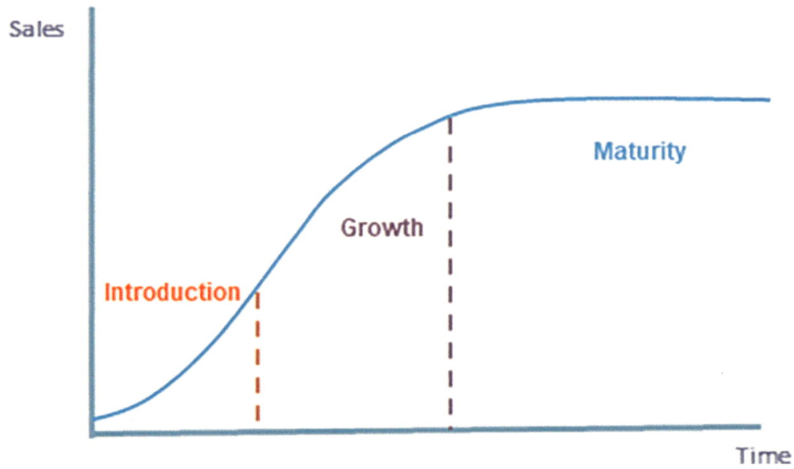

Figure 1.
Development of the business over time. Source: Prepared by the author.

market and the sales growth rate decreases, it is known that the company has entered the ***maturity stage***. This can be seen in **Figure 1**, which corresponds to the development of the business over time, which since its introduction has seen sales grow with an S-shaped trend line inclined forward.

1.2 Incorporation of a new stage in the business life cycle

In business theory, the introduction, growth and maturity stages of the business life cycle are established[1]; however, based on the observations of the evolution of the companies, it is considered important to incorporate an additional stage: **the stage of business development**. In this period, the products are formed until the moment where they are incorporated into the company's sales, generating the first income. **Figure 2** shows this stage where the investments are mainly made, which will

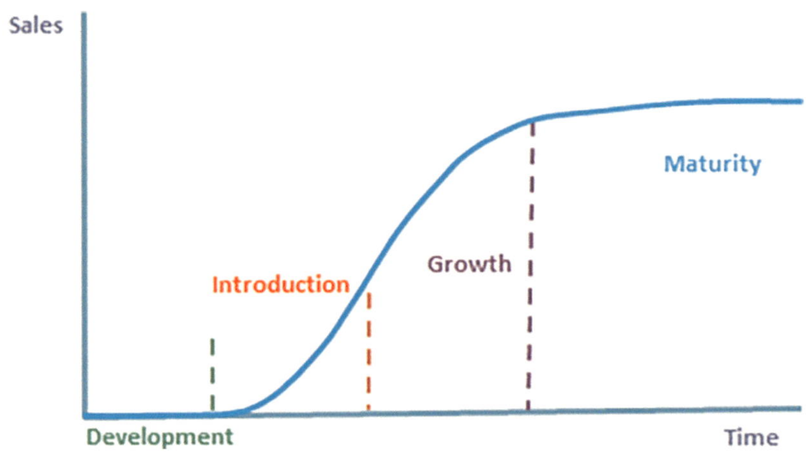

Figure 2.
The stage of business development. Source: Prepared by the author.

[1] From the concepts of product life cycle.

Figure 3.
Investment and first income. Source: Prepared by the author.

be extended over time depending on the business that is being developed, closely related to the type of innovation involved in the company's products. The incorporation of the development stage will make it possible to use the business life cycle in terms of the evolution of investments, its Income Statements and Cash Flows.

The development stage results in a series of investment flows until the company achieves a minimum viable product (MVP) that can be sold in the market. From this, the first sales and, consequently, the first income are achieved, thus starting the introduction stage of the business life cycle, as shown in **Figure 3**. Then the familiar stages of the business life cycle will follow.

1.3 The development of revenue in a business valuation model

For a company valuation process, it must begin with the projection of sales or income, since, as previously mentioned, these will define the construction and expected evolution of the Income Statements and Economic Flows, which are used in the two most widely used business valuation methods. According to Fernandez "to value a company with expectations of continuity, it is based on the discount of fund flows, with which the company is considered as a flow-generating entity" [1]. In this sense, for an existing company, income can be projected from the historical information found in the financial statements of past periods. However, in new companies such as startups, the evolution of sales or income must be built based on market studies or taking businesses from the same sector or with similar business units as a reference. The latter is typical of technological businesses in which this document focuses.

Thus, for example, we establish that after the **development stage** (between period 0 and 3) of the products of the startup being analyzed, sales of the product begin in period 4, which grow moderately during the **introduction stage**. It is expected that the market will accept the product from periods 9 or 10 and there will be high sales growth rates until around period 18 -where the **growth stage** would end- a period

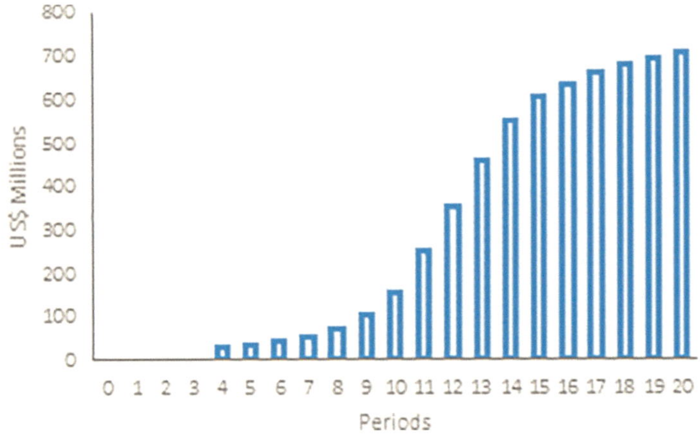

Figure 4.
Sales. Source: Prepared by the author.

with moderate growth rates is entered, establishing the **maturity stage**. This description of the business life cycle through the evolution of expected sales can be seen in **Figure 4**.

The products or services will be sold at the price or rate established according to market conditions, based on the products to be replaced or the market's willingness to pay. Consequently, the behavior of the income will be defined, which will have a behavior similar to the evolution of sales. **Figure 5** shows the evolution of sales and income, in a double scale Graph to appreciate that they have the same trend.

1.4 The relationship between the income and the projected costs and expenses

After projecting income, the evolution of costs and expenses must be projected, concepts that are closely related, because although they do not vary perfectly

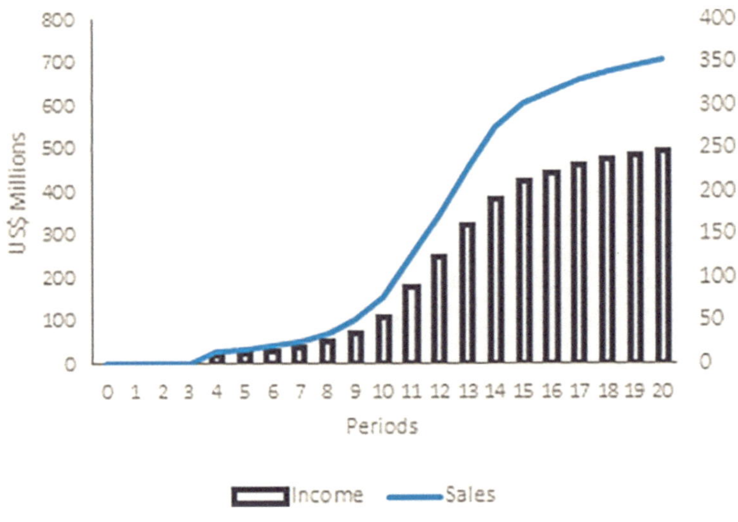

Figure 5.
Sales and income. Source: Prepared by the author.

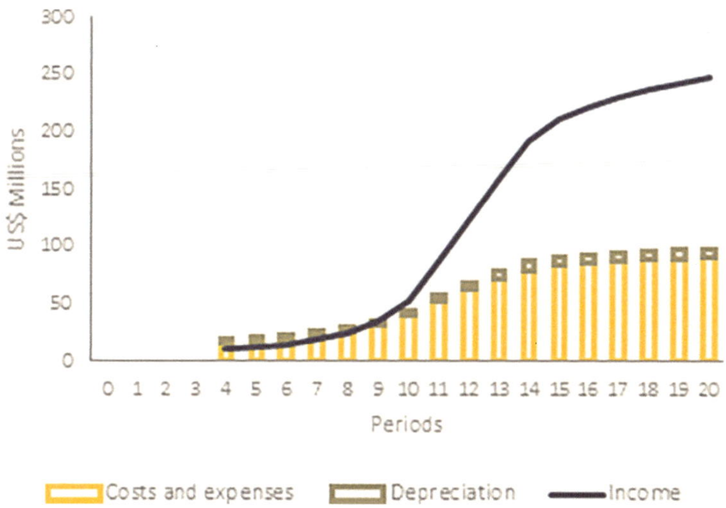

Figure 6.
Income, costs and expenses. Source: Prepared by the author.

proportionally, costs and expenses evolve in the same direction as income. On the one hand, fixed or semi-fixed costs will have to be projected, which have a stable behavior for a period of time, but grow over time with the increase in the company's capacity; on the other hand, there are variable costs that do evolve proportionally to income.

The projection of the expenses shows a behavior similar to the semi-fixed costs, the projection of the depreciation -or amortizations- is also carried out,[2] which will depend on the investments made in the development stage and the additional investments in fixed assets. In **Figure 6** it can be seen that in several periods -from 4 to 8- costs and expenses are greater than income despite the fact that the company has sales. This happens, because to achieve sales targets, the company must have a production capacity prepared to support growth and an organization that drives sales so that revenue forecasts are met. This means that initially the income cannot cover the costs until a certain moment in which the break-even point is achieved. It is expected that, from then on, revenues will grow at a higher rate than costs and expenses.

1.5 The profit projection

To project the profits, the Income Statements are built in the valuation horizon, as shown in **Figure 7**, finding the difference between the Income and the Costs and Expenses, which will result in the projection of Profit Before Taxes for each period. If this is positive, then the income tax is calculated, which the company must pay to the treasury, in the corresponding period; if it resulted in a loss then the tax would not be paid in that period.[3]

---

[2] Depreciation corresponds to tangible fixed assets, while amortization corresponds to intangible fixed assets.

[3] A loss can be used as a credit for future income tax payments, this benefit is regulated according to the tax legislation in each country.

Income Statement	202...
Sales revenue	
(Costs and expenses)	
(Depreciation)	
Profit before Taxes	
(Income tax)	
Net profit	

Figure 7.
Statements of Income. Source: Prepared by the author.

As previously seen, between periods 4 and 8 costs and expenses are higher than sales revenue; consequently, it will be observed that there will be losses in each of these periods. Subsequently, in period 9, the income manages to exceed costs and expenses and there is a growth in profits following the pattern of the business life cycle; that is to say, that there is a notable growth rate in the growth stage and then it slows down until it has a more modest rate in the maturity stage, as see in **Figure 8**. In these periods of profit before positive taxes, the corresponding income taxes will be paid.

It is highly probable that, in the initial stage of the company, losses will be obtained by not obtaining sufficient income to cover its costs and expenses; however, a situation of losses could be maintained for a long time, since an organization is still proportionally large for the initial income. This scenario will be reflected in the need to make additional investments to sustain the business until the moment where profits are achieved (*break-even point*) and then have a surplus cash flow, where income is greater than expenses; which is generally achieved in the final stage of growth and especially in the stage of maturity. According to Tsorakidis, et al. Break-Even Point is

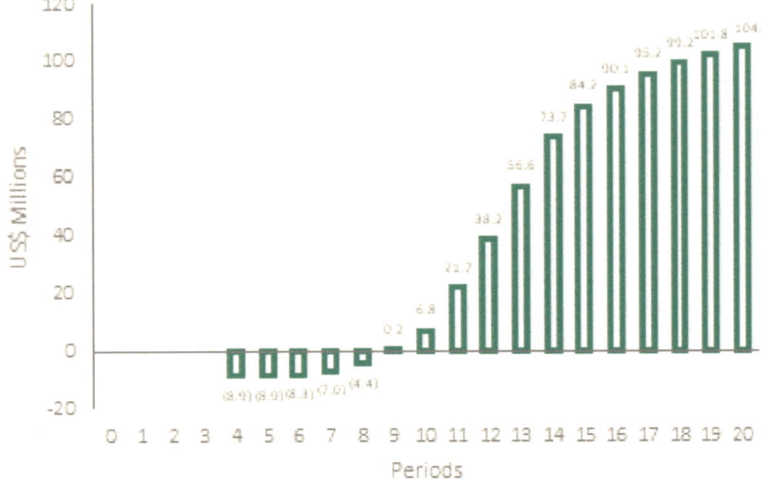

Figure 8.
Profit. Source: Prepared by the author.

determined as the point at which total sales revenues are equal to total expenses (both fixed and variable). That is, it is the point that corresponds to this level of production capacity, under which the company operates at loss [2].

In the company valuation process, having an overview of the evolution of profits is important because it allows identifying the representative profit that will be used in the net profit valuation method, which will be explained later.

1.6 The projection of the economic cash flow

The other most widely used method for company valuation is the discounted cash flow method, which consists of updating the company's projected economic flows. To build the economic flow, the company's operating cash flow, investments in fixed assets and investments in working capital must be projected. The operating cash flow is the difference between income and expenses of each period, where the income is the same as that which has been considered in the Income Statement, similarly the expenses are the costs and expenses of the same financial statement, with the difference that the cash flow does not consider the depreciation or amortization of tangible or intangible fixed assets, as appropriate. The operating cash flow is subtracted from the investments in fixed assets and working capital that are made in the first periods - from 0 to 3- and the additional investments that are projected to be executed in the operational stage of the company. These last investments are necessary to support the growth in sales, since they imply increasing the capacity of fixed assets and a greater contribution of working capital to finance higher costs and expenses of incremental sales. The structure of the economic flow can be seen in **Figure 9**.

In **Figure 10**, you can see the preoperative stage where only investments are made—period 0 to 3—; subsequently, the operational stage begins with the first sales, but for a period of time—from 4 to 10 it is not possible to have a sufficient operating cash flow to finance investments in fixed assets and investments in working capital; finally, the stage is reached where the cash flow is surplus and therefore can cover the necessary investments.

In the economic cash flow of the previous Graph, it can be seen that there is an extensive period of negative economic flows that represents investments to be made, and from period 11, positive economic flows are obtained that grow in the same configuration as the cycle of life of the business or sales, which from a stage of growth

Economic flow	**202...**
Sales revenue (Costs and expenses) (Income tax)	
Operating Cash Flow (Fixed Asset Investments) (Working Capital Investments	
Economic flow	

Figure 9.
Economic flow. Source: Prepared by the author.

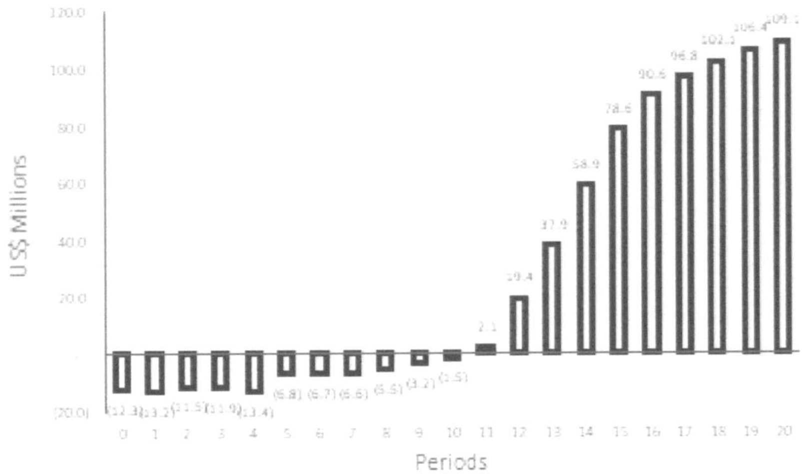

Figure 10.
Projection of the economic flow. Source: Prepared by the author.

passes to a stage of maturity. This process is important, since it indicates that in the end the cash flow will have a value that grows at a moderate rate, important data for the treatment of perpetuities in the valuation process.

1.7 Profit projections and economic flow in the valuation of a startup

In the case of startups, despite the fact that they may imply long investment periods, loss statements and negative cash flows, businesses have value and this can be surprisingly high, since from the beginning and during the course of During these periods, investors observe the potential of the business by evaluating the business projections for the future, considering that the value of the business will be given by the profits—and positive cash flows—when they occur in the future.

When new companies (startups) are valued, it is important to visualize their life cycle, since they generally take time to generate profits or positive cash flows, which is why the investment stage and the moment when they prove their viability as businesses are prolonged. However, for the valuation of companies it is important to identify the moment in which they are expected to generate profits or positive economic flows.

So when they seek to obtain economic resources in business meetings to implement their idea or carry out an IPO (*Initial Public Offering*) for their business consolidation, the business life cycle must be projected and the expectations of income, profits and flows must be shown in each one of those moments. Now, it is important to mention that not all startups have similar life cycles. For example, start-ups that correspond to businesses based on the intensive use of technologies generally show a tendency to have a longer duration of the investment stage, since the introduction stage is slow; however, if they manage to be successful ventures, they have rapid growth and achieve greater market dimensions, until they reach the maturity stage.

From the point of view of the type of technological innovation, businesses can be classified into different dimensions, although for the purpose of projecting the economic states and flows of the business it is considered important to distinguish between process innovations—or frugal innovation—and disruptive innovations.

What is relevant about this distinction is that it will be possible to observe different durations of the stages of the life cycle of these businesses.

In businesses that break through with disruptive innovations, the introduction stage is usually longer, since as they are innovative products, market approval must be awaited; however, once this happens, the growth rate is expected to be high. It also happens that the dimension of the disruptive business market is greater compared to frugal innovations, since the latter optimize processes of broader production chains, so that the latter find their maturation stage in less time.

1.8 Business valuation methods

The financial value of a company, or more precisely the financial value of Shareholders' Equity, represented in **Figure 11**, is what the market is willing to pay for the purchase or sale of the company, proportionally to the shares of the company. This can be represented in the company's Balance Sheet, where the accounting Equity - which represents what is invested by the shareholders- takes a value based on the benefits of the business, if it is good and generates high profits, then the financial value of the equity It will be higher than the book value, but if the business does not have good prospects it can even reach a lower book value.

The valuation of shareholders' equity or market capitalization serves as the basis for purchase and sale transactions of shares of minority positions, where the price per share is equivalent to the market capitalization divided by the number of shares.

$$Price\ per\ Share = \frac{Market\ capitalization}{Number\ of\ Shares} \tag{1}$$

The market capitalization is formed based on the expected earnings of the company and is then reflected in the price per share. For this reason, in the capital market, the net income method is used to determine the value of equity and shares.

When the valuation is carried out, for example, for the purpose of buying or selling a company, then it is necessary to have greater strength in measuring the evolution of the company's net income and it may even be necessary to carry out Due Diligence

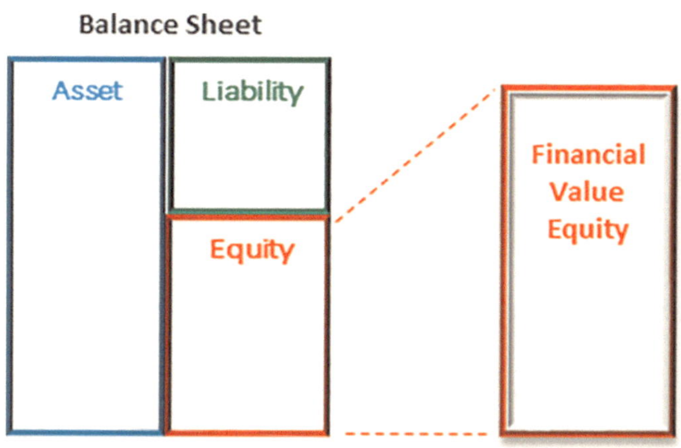

Figure 11.
Company balance sheet. Source: Prepared by the author.

processes to ensure that the determination of the fundamentals is correct. In this case, the discounted cash flow valuation method is the most appropriate.

Next, two useful methodologies will be developed to value start-ups.

1.8.1 Valuation by Income Statements (Net Income)

To estimate the financial value of shareholders' equity, it is necessary to project the expected profit of the business, which must be representative of the business. Then the one who values must project the Income Statement, analyzing the evolution of income and costs, distinguishing the company's fixed and variable costs, which will depend on the particular characteristics of the company's operation. Then, administrative expenses and provisions for depreciation or amortization of assets must be projected. The resulting Net Profit, after taxes, will give us the information to calculate the value of the shareholders' equity.

In **Figure 12**, the Balance Sheet of the NLS company, an investment of $12.3 MM is being considered, which is financed entirely with sources of capital or equity. In the case of startups, financing basically comes from capital contributions, since the company in formation is not subject to credit and therefore does not access debt financing. This will also be reflected in the projection of the Income Statement, since financial expenses will not be considered, since the company will not pay interest on debt.[4]

If the NLS Income Statement is developed, as shown in **Figure 13**, the income ($88.1 MM), costs and expenses of the company ($52.4 MM), as well as the depreciation ($4.7 MM) of tangible fixed assets can be established in which the company has invested. From the difference between costs and expenses, there is a profit before taxes ($31.0 MM), which at a tax rate of 30% results in income tax ($9.3 MM), to finally obtain a net profit ($21.7MM).

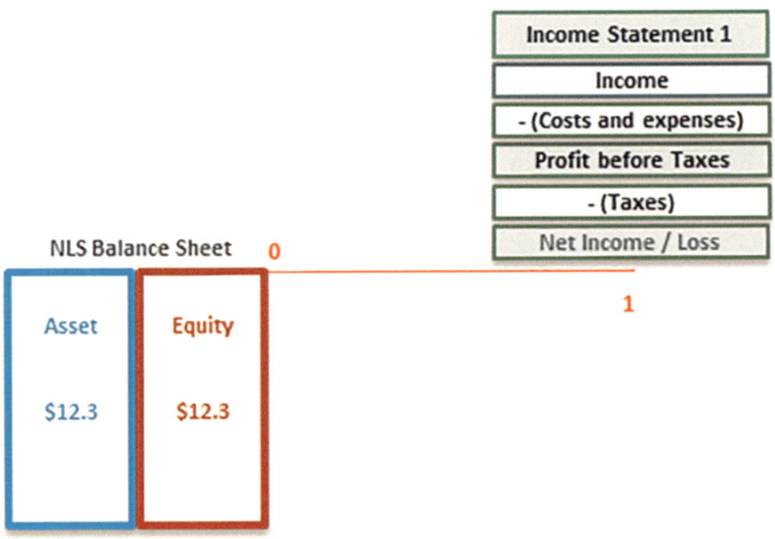

Figure 12.
NLS balance sheet. Source: Prepared by the author.

[4] In the valuations of companies that have access to credit, the liabilities must be considered in the Balance Sheet and the financial expenses in the Income Statement.

Income Statement	1
Sales revenue	88.1
(Costs and expenses)	(52.4)
(Depreciation)	(4.7)
Profit before Taxes	31.0
(Income tax)(30%)	(9.3)
Net profit	21.7

Figure 13.
Income Statement. Source: Prepared by the author.

g	3.0%

	1	2	3	4	5	6	7	8	9	10
Net profit	21.7	22.3	23.0	23.7	24.4	25.2	25.9	26.7	27.5	28.3

Figure 14.
Perpetuity growth at 3%.

For the valuation process, it is considered that a series of net profits is obtained over time, forming a perpetuity from period 1 ($21.7 MM) and that period by period it grows at a certain rate (3%). A series of 10 periods is presented in **Figures 14** and **15**, however, it is considered that net profits grow in perpetuity.[5]

In order to determine the financial value of the patrimony, this series of profits must be updated following the following formula;

$$Present\ Value = \frac{Net\ profit\ 1}{K - g} \tag{2}$$

Where:

Net Income 1	Corresponds to the profit of the initial period of the series of net profits ($21.7 MM).
K	It is the shareholder's cost of capital that corresponds to the business risk (8%).
g	Is the growth rate of net profit (3%)

Consequently, the Present Value of the perpetuity of the net income of $21.7 MM of a business that has a cost of capital of 8% and that grows at 3% will be $433.9 MM (see **Figure 16**).

[5] The use of perpetuities is almost equivalent to using a 40 or 50 year series, since the present value of net income or any cash flow located in those years forward is less and less significant.

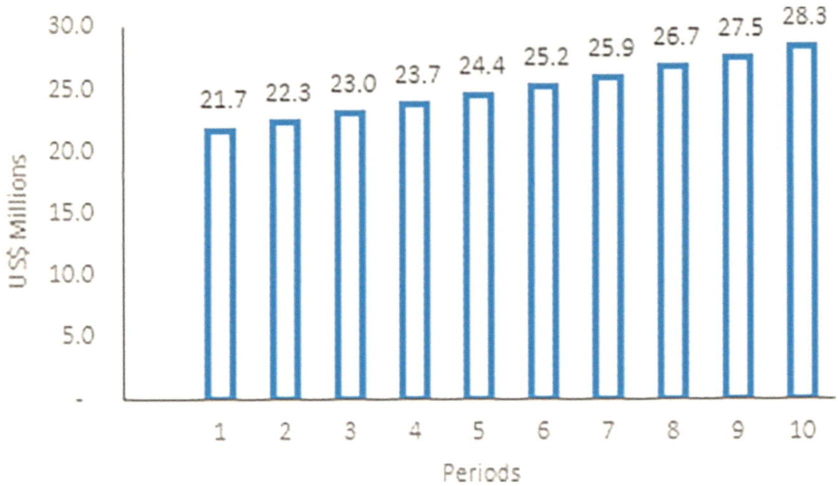

Figure 15.
Net profit. Source: Prepared by the author.

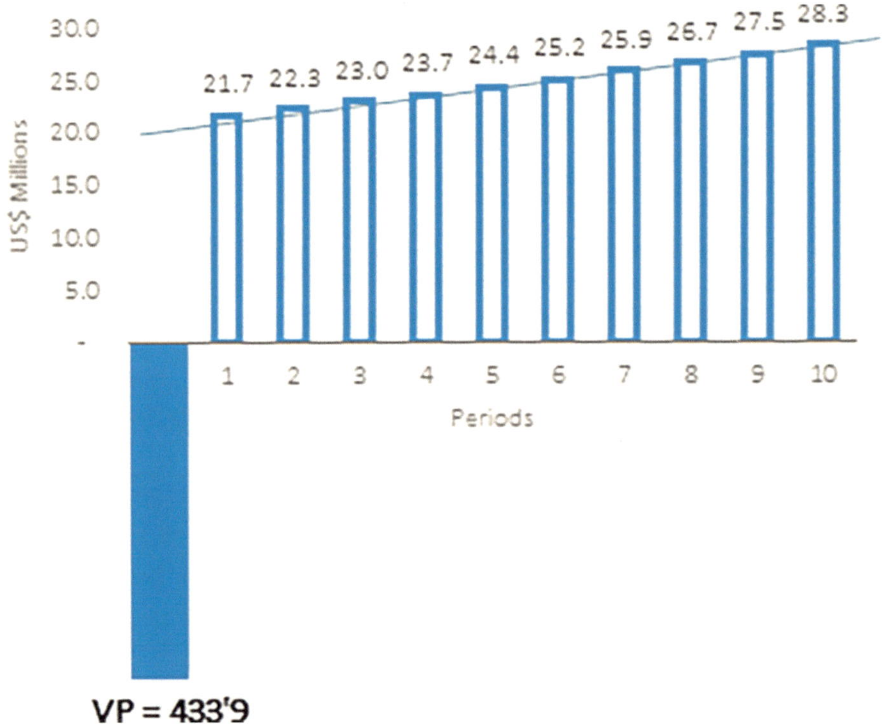

Figure 16.
Net profit and present value. Source: Prepared by the author.

$$Present\ \ Value = \frac{\$21'7}{8\% - 3\%} = \$433'9 \tag{3}$$

Then, in the absence of debt financing, the Financial Value of the Equity will be \$433.9 MM and will be located in the initial period 0, as shown in **Figure 17**.

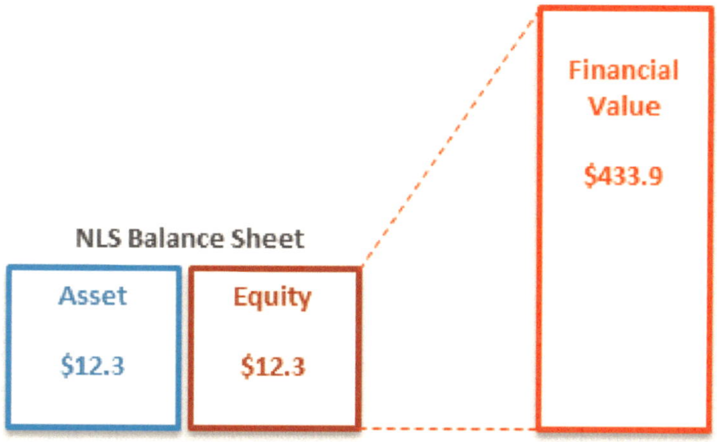

Figure 17.
Financial value of the equity. Source: Prepared by the author.

1.8.2 The PER method

In the market or stock market, the names of the components of the valuation formula are usually varied; however, the concepts that determine the valuation through the net profit method are maintained. The formula that is being used is the updating of the Net Profit of period 1 that grows at g% and the series of profits is discounted at the cost of capital K.

$$Equity\ Value = P_0 = \frac{UN_1}{K-g} \tag{4}$$

That same formula can be expressed by separating the Net Profit (UN1) from the quotient $\frac{1}{K-g}$, leaving it as follows:

$$P_0 = \frac{1}{K-g}\ x\ UN_1 \tag{5}$$

The quotient $\frac{1}{K-g}$ is renamed as the Price/Earnings Ratio or the PER (Price-to-Earnings Ratio) multiplier so that the formula for calculating the Equity Value is expressed as a multiple of the Net Income. This is the formula that is applied in the stock market, but as can be seen, it is the same that corresponds to the net profit method.

$$P_0 = PER\ x\ UN_1 \tag{6}$$

Then the PER could be calculated that corresponds to a cost of capital of 8% and a growth rate of profits of 3%.

$$PER = \frac{1}{K-g} = \frac{1}{8\% - 3\%} = 20 \tag{7}$$

Thus we will have that the equity value can be calculated by multiplying the Net Profit by the PER, obtaining the same equity value:

$$P_0 = PER\ x\ UN_1 = 20\ x\ \$21'7 = \$433'9 \tag{8}$$

However, the use of the PER is made more frequently on the price per share, which initially results from dividing the Equity Value by the number of shares, which results in $8.97/share.

$$\begin{aligned} Price\ per\ share &= \frac{Equity\ Value}{Number\ of\ shares} \\ p_0 = \frac{P_0}{\#Acc} &= \frac{\$433'9}{48'4} = \$8.97/Shares \end{aligned} \tag{9}$$

The Equity Value formula could be expressed in the price per share by dividing the equity value and net income by the number of shares. Then the formula for the price per share based on the PER multiplier (20) times the earnings per share ($0.448/share) will be obtained, which will result in the same value of the price per share of $8.97/share.

$$\begin{aligned} P_0 = PER\ x\ UN_1 \rightarrow \frac{p_0}{\#Acc} &= PER\ x\ \frac{upa_1}{\#Acc} \\ p_0 &= PER\ x\ upa_1 \\ p_0 = 20\ x\ \$0.448/shares &= \$8.97/shares \end{aligned} \tag{10}$$

1.8.3 The net income in the life cycle of a startup

In calculating the Equity Value, it has been assumed that the Net Income of $21.7 MM was in period 1 and from that period it grew at a rate of 3%, however, as can be seen in the **Figure 18**, In the initial periods there are losses in each annual exercise and then small profits until reaching a profit of $21.7 MM in period 12.

Then the Equity Value determined previously is located in period 10 and not in the initial period 0. In the following Graph 14 it can be clearly seen that the update of the

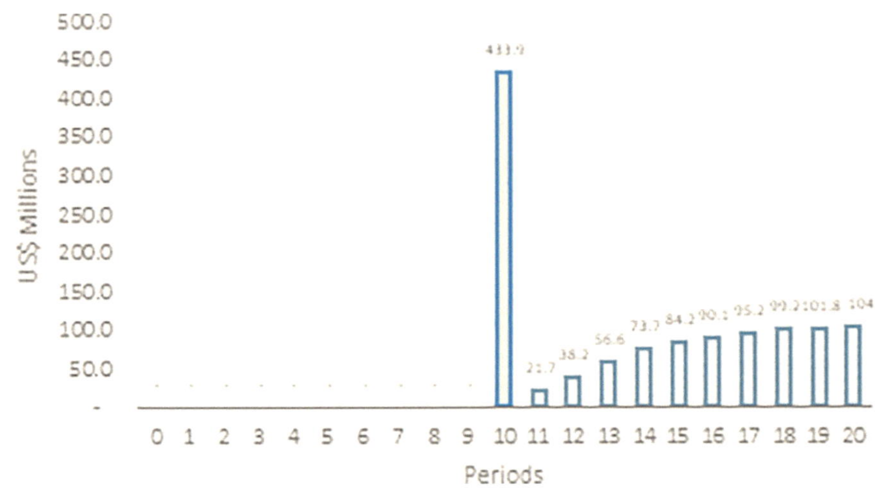

Figure 18.
Net profits updated at present value. Source: Prepared by the author.

series of net profits that begins with UN $_{11}$ of \$21.7 MM, generates a Present Value in period 10 (PV $_{01}$) of \$433.9 MM.

This Present Value at period 10 will be the Financial Value of the Shareholders' Equity, which will be related to the rights of the shareholders for that period. Once the business and equity have been valued, this value can be expressed in period 0, for which they must be updated together with the investments made up to the time of valuation (period 10) and thus have the value of equity in the initial period.

However, this financial value of the equity (located for the example in period 10), which is shown in **Figure 19**, is usually used to determine the right of the different shareholders that are added to the company, such as the initial promoters, venture capital funds, among others.

1.8.4 The life cycle and valuation by discounted cash flows

The discounted cash flow valuation method begins with the determination of the projected economic flows of the business, which unite the investment flows in fixed assets and in contributions -or increases in working capital-, as well as the cash flows that are observed in **Figure 10**.

As can be seen in **Figure 20**, the economic flows are negative until period 9 and then they become positive and gradually grow until their growth rate decreases in the maturity stage, thus following the development of the business life cycle. This extended period of the business development stage corresponds to disruptive innovation businesses; however, in each case they can be varied periods. As can also be identified in the previous economic flow, the first investment to be made is \$12.3 MM and if we assume that the valuation will be carried out after having made this first capital contribution, we would have that the opening General Balance would be established with this investment and economic flows would be expected to occur from period 1 onwards.

Once the investment has been made, the financial value of the equity will be determined by updating the economic flows at a discount rate that in most cases is the

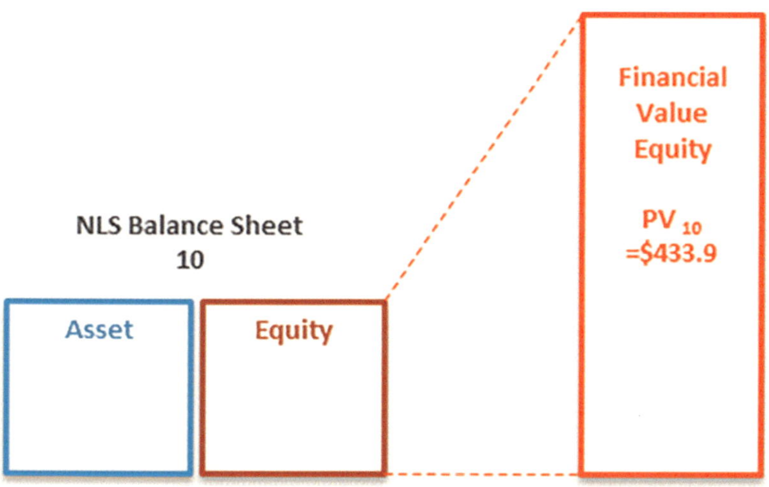

Figure 19.
Financial value of the equity (located for the example in period 10). Source: Prepared by the author.

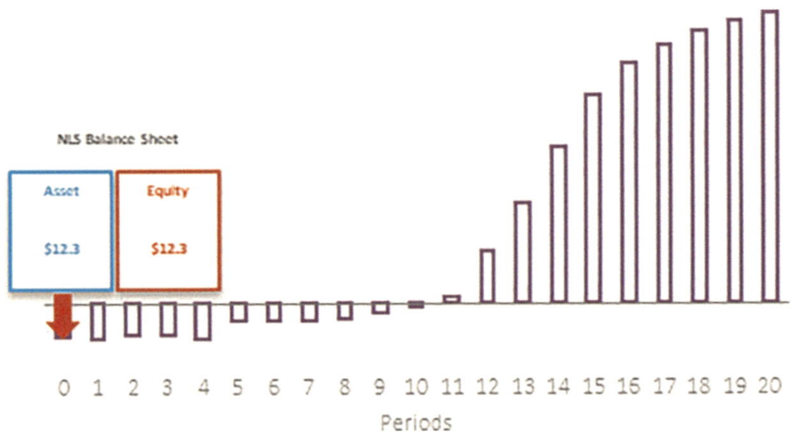

Figure 20.
Economic flow. Source: Prepared by the author.

weighted average cost of capital[6] (Ko), which in this case is 12%, as it can be seen in **Figure 21**. Initially we will assume that the economic flows reach period 20 to later incorporate the effect of perpetuity. Thus, using the formula of the Net Present Value of Excel, where the economic flows and the discount rate are incorporated, the Present Value of the economic flows will be determined.

$$VP\ Economics\ Flows = VNA\ (Ko, FE_1FE_2FE_3 \ldots \ldots \ldots \ldots FE_{19}FE_{20}) \tag{11}$$

From the extract of the spreadsheet presented in **Figure 22**, it can be verified that the Present Value of the economic flows between the periods 1 to 20 is $54.5 MM, which will be located in the initial period 0. This value represents the net value of the update of all flows up to period 20.

Consequently, as shown in **Figure 23**, it will be necessary that the flow of the business throughout its life cycle is producing a value of $54.5 MM greater than the initial investment of $12.3 MM, which establishes the possibility of generating added value over the initial investment.

		1	2	3	4	5	...	20
Economic flow		(13.2)	(11.5)	(11.9)	(13.4)	(6.8)	...	109.1
Ko	12%							
VP								
FE	4.5							

Figure 21.
Present value of economic flows. Source: Prepared by the author.

---

[6] Since the startup is assuming no debt, the weighted average cost will be the shareholder opportunity cost of capital.

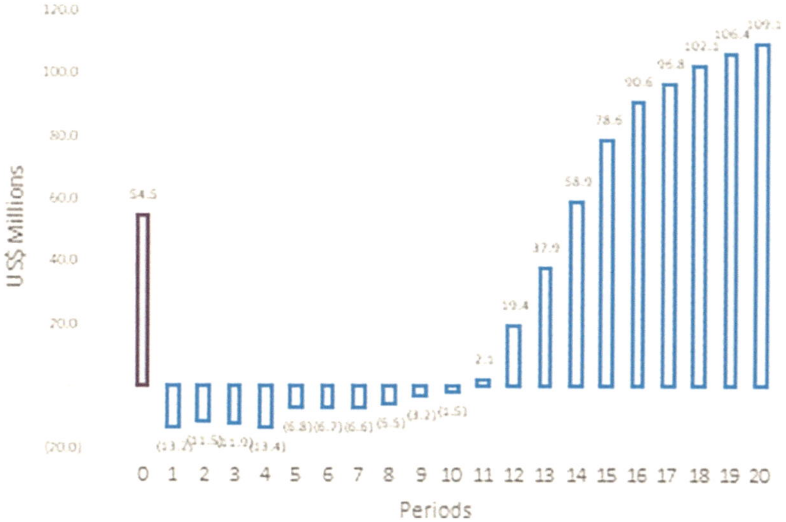

Figure 22.
The net value of the update of all flows up to period 20. Source: Prepared by the author.

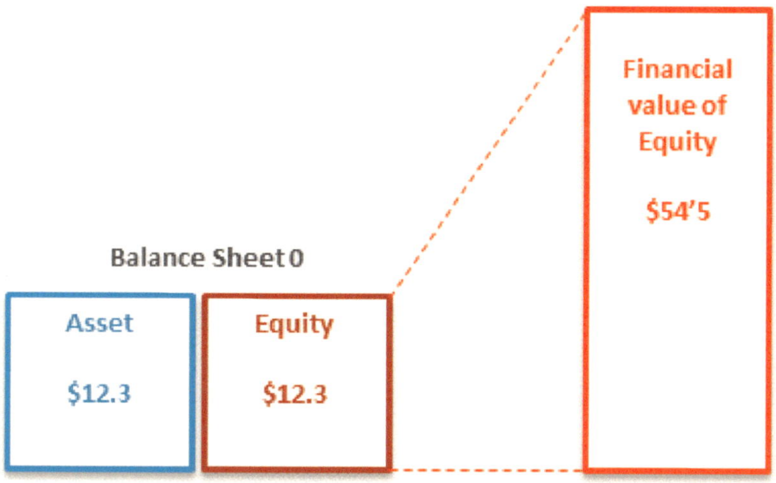

Figure 23.
Generation of added value. Source: Prepared by the author.

1.8.5 The effect of perpetuities

In business valuation, the life cycle of the business generally extends for several years after its maturity stage. However, when using the perpetuity method, it is important to be sure that the business being valued is expected to have a duration of at least 40 years.[7]

---

[7] A 40-year period is considered since the Present Value of a 40-year economic flow is similar to the present value using the perpetuity method.

In the maturity stage, the growth rate of economic flows is approaching an almost vegetative growth, which in the case being analyzed is considered a g of 3%. Consequently, the Perpetuity Value can be determined as follows.

$$
\begin{aligned}
VP\ FE\ Perpetual_{20} &= \frac{FE_{21}}{Ko - g} \\
VP\ FE\ Perpetual_{20} &= \frac{FE_{20}\ (1 + Ko)}{Ko - g} = \frac{109.1\ (1 + 12\%)}{12\% - 3\%} = 1{,}357.8
\end{aligned}
\tag{12}
$$

The Present Value of the perpetual economic flow is found updating the flows that begin the following period, 21,[8] which is discounted at the difference between the discount rate and the growth rate. To calculate the economic flow of period 21, the economic flow of period 20 is taken and carried to 21. Thus, it is finally obtained that the Present Value of the perpetuity for period 20 is equivalent to $1357.8 MM, as presented in **Figure 24**.

The value of the perpetuity determined from the last economic flow of period 20 ($1357.8 MM) is added to the economic flow of period 20 ($109.1 MM), obtaining a total flow of $1466.9 MM, as shown in **Figure 25**.

Then, in **Figure 26**, using a discount rate of 12%, the economic flow that considers the value of the perpetuity is updated and thus the Present Value of the economic flows is determined, which amounts to $195.2 MM.

	17	18	19	20
Economic flow	96.8	102.1	106.4	109.1
				1,357.8
Economic flow	96.8	102.1	106.4	1,466.9
			Ko	12%
			g	3%

Figure 24.
The Present Value of the perpetuity for period 20. Source: Prepared by the author.

		1	2	...	17	18	19	20
Economic flow		(13.2)	(11.5)	...	96.8	102.1	106.4	109.1
								1,357.8
Economic flow		(13.2)	(11.5)	...	96.8	102.1	106.4	1,466.9
Ko	12%						Ko	12%
VP FE	195.2						g	3%

Figure 25.
Total flow. Source: Prepared by the author.

---

[8] Assuming that they continue to infinity (in practice 40 years).

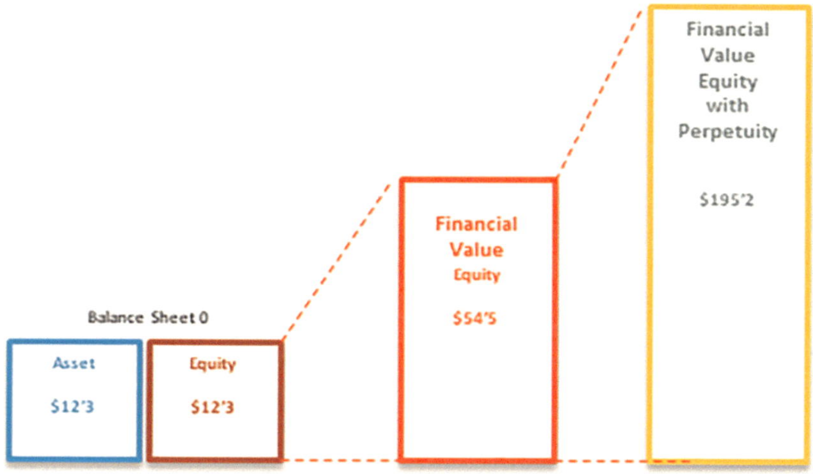

Figure 26.
Present value of the economic flows. Source: Prepared by the author.

Considering an evaluation horizon of 20 periods, the Equity Valuation results in $54.5 MM and if the value of the perpetuity of economic flows is considered, the value increases to $195.2. Note that it is a significant increase, so it is important to keep in mind for the use of perpetuity that the business must reach at least 40 years or a discount rate must be considered that incorporates the little certainty that the business will mature. It is also important to determine the growth rate of economic flows (g), since this value can strongly modify the present value of the perpetuity.

1.8.6 Identifying differentiated discount rates

The capital costs that can be obtained in the market are generally from companies in progress and with a history of operating in the market, this is not the case of startups because by definition they are new companies that need investments in their stage of development. Development and in the introduction stage, even in part of the growth stage. These are periods where it is not yet possible to obtain profits or positive economic flows. Consequently, what must be done is separate the updating of the economic flows into two stages, one where the flows already reflect the consolidation of the business and another where the flows show that greater net investments are still being made.

The consolidation stage is from period 11 where the first positive economic flow is achieved and from then on it can be considered that the business is growing, which then enters maturity and finally has a perpetuity behavior with growth of g%. Then you can start to replace the average rate of 12% with a cost of capital of 9%, an expected return that corresponds to similar businesses but that are already in the market. With this modification, the value of the perpetuity of the flows from period 21 onwards increases from $1357.8 MM to $1982.2 (see **Figure 27**).

Since the idea is to have the value of the business at the stage where it could be similar to a business of the same type but that is already on the market, then we discount the positive economic flows from period 11 to 20, which includes the perpetuity value considering that this update is made at the cost of capital or expected

	17	18	19	20
Economic flow	96.8	102.1	106.4	109.1
				1,982.2
Economic flow	96.8	102.1	106.4	2,091.3
			Ko	9%
			g	3%

Figure 27.
New perpetuity value. Source: Prepared by the author.

return of 9%. Thus, the Present Value of the business is obtained $1231 MM, which will be located in period 10 and which represents the value of the business when the investments have already been made, as shown in **Figure 28**.

Then the economic flows from period 1 to 10 are updated, which includes the Present Value of the flows from 11 to 20, including perpetuity. **Figure 29** shows that, in this period a discount rate of 20% higher than the 9% that corresponds to the business consolidation stage is used. The reason is because at this stage investors assume the risk of the company's *default* without being sure of being able to reach the period where profits or positive flows begin to be generated, so this risk assessment derives in the use of a high expected return.

From the update, there is a Present Value of the economic flows of $157.5 MM that considers the effect of the perpetuities and the discount rates in stages and that can be seen in the **Figure 30**.

	9	10	11	12	13	14	15	16	17	18	19	20
Economic flow	(3.2)	(1.5)	2.1	19.4	37.9	58.9	78.6	90.6	96.8	102.1	106.4	109.1
												1,982
Economic flow	(3.2)	(1.5)	2.1	19.4	37.9	58.9	78.6	90.6	96.8	102.1	106.4	2,091
											Ko	9%
											g	3%

Figure 28.
The Present Value of the business. Source: Prepared by the author.

	1	2	3	4	5	6	7	8	9	10
Economic flow	(13.2)	(11.5)	(11.9)	(13.4)	(6.8)	(6.7)	(6.6)	(5.5)	(3.2)	(1.5)
Economic flow	(13.2)	(11.5)	(11.9)	(13.4)	(6.8)	(6.7)	(6.6)	(5.5)	(3.2)	(1.5)
Ko 20%									Ko	9%
VP FE 157.5									VP FE	1,231.0

Figure 29.
Economic flow from 1 to 10 with perpetuity (11–20). Source: Prepared by the author.

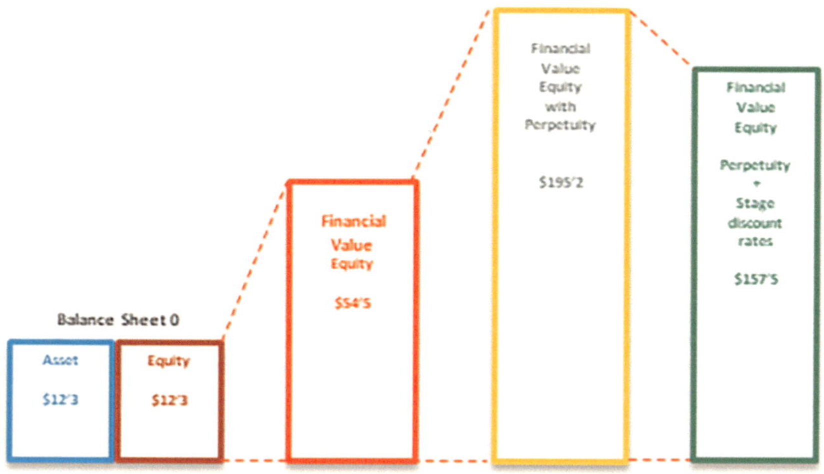

Figure 30.
Effect of the perpetuities and the discount rates. Source: Prepared by the author.

2. Startups by type of innovation

Schumpeter highlighted the leading role of innovation as a fundamental internal engine for the economic growth of companies and nations. Therefore, regardless of the origin of the companies, the innovation of processes, products and services constitutes a strategy that allows companies to project greater added value, increasing the possibilities that they can become competitive organizations and manage to adapt to the demands of world markets.

For Schmookler, innovation arises after the need to solve a problem, creative and innovative ideas respond to a demand originating in the environment [3]. Sherman [4] defines innovation as Ideas originated after identifying a need, resulting in the invention of new products, processes or techniques to achieve success in the market. Malerba and Orsenigo define innovation as a dynamic and interrelated process, with continuous feedback effects between the different stages, and, furthermore, this entire process takes place in a changing environment in which agents and competitors react, in turn, before each of the changes [5]. Likewise, the OECD defines innovation as the creation or improvement of a product, process or in turn the combination of both [6].

There are various authors who have defined innovation; however, in most definitions it is understood that innovation is associated with the use of knowledge for the creation of strategies capable of generating improvements in the product or process. For this reason, process innovation and disruptive innovation will be defined below.

2.1 Process innovation or frugal innovation

When you talk about innovation, you have the preconceived idea that it means the creation of a totally new product; however, innovation could also occur in the modification of a current process to make it more efficient. This is known as process innovation -or frugal innovation- and consists of the application of knowledge that develops new tools or methodologies that allow optimizing the behavior and results of the processes ([7], p. 19).

Through process innovation, companies manage to increase their competitiveness, reducing costs and times, improving customer satisfaction rates. In this way, the returns on investment are increased and the participation of the company in the market is increased ([7], p. 23).

Process innovation must meet certain conditions to be considered as such. This type of innovation must increase the productivity or yields obtained so far and there must be a significant and demonstrable change, otherwise, it cannot be considered as innovation, but as an improvement in the process, also called Kaizen (see **Figure 31**).

The kaizen method has the same objectives as innovation in terms of increasing competitiveness; however, this is achieved through the constant improvement of the business productive apparatus. That is, through "small improvements made in the status quo as a result of progressive efforts" ([7], p. 31), while innovation implies a drastic improvement in the status quo.

2.2 Disruptive innovation

Various academics such as Danneels [8], Bass [9], among others, define disruptive innovation as the evolution of a product or service, using technologies to increase current returns. This causes companies that go through this process to displace established competitors. This type of innovation has as its main characteristic the transformation potential of industries and considers the process from the introduction of changes to the acceptance of the new offer in the market by new consumers [10].

For disruption to be successful, it must have the potential to improve steadily over time; For this reason, the innovation process includes "subsequent developments that raise the attributes of the new product to a level sufficient to satisfy the main customers" ([11], p. 13; [12]). **Figure 32** shows the fundamental characteristics of disruptive innovation.

2.3 Compared life cycle of startups

2.3.1 Differences in risk

All companies face constant challenges that put business stability at risk. Companies that decide to innovate are not exempt from these dangers. For this reason, this section will discuss the main types of risks faced by companies that are committed to innovation.

The implementation of any innovative idea requires previous studies that evaluate the feasibility, development of the prototype, the business model, among other previous steps, which represent an investment in research and development. Even, on some occasions, transferring the innovation from the prototype to reality is highly expensive and sometimes it is not possible to have a viable product or that the market can demand, so the investment made is risky.

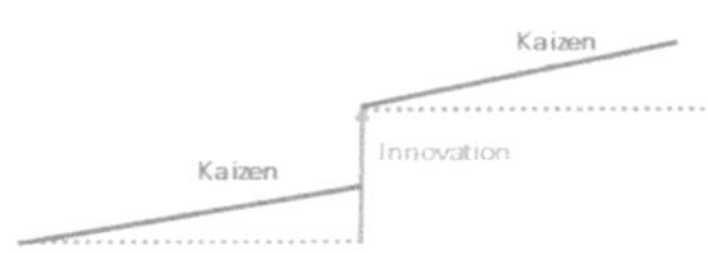

Figure 31.
Differences between Kaizen and innovation. Source: [7].

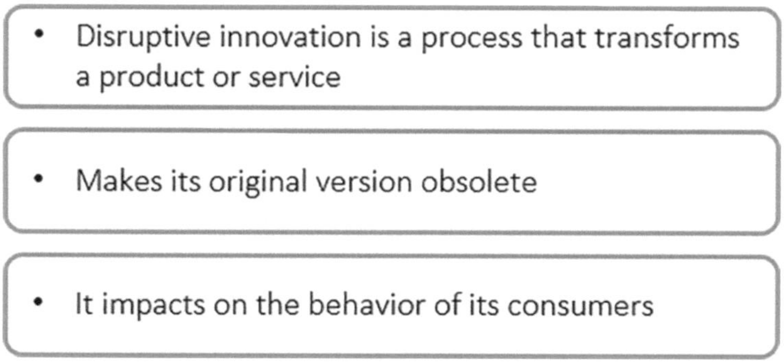

Figure 32.
Subsequent developments that raise the attributes. Source: Prepared by the author.

As for companies that choose to innovate in their processes, most of the risk is found in the Research, development and implementation process, since it is at this stage that the greatest investment is needed. On the other hand, disruptive innovation is conditioned by a type of additional risk, given that, once the implementation investment has been made, the product or service may not be well received in the market. Disruptive innovations usually have unattractive performance in the short term, since they assume a different value than the one established, so that new products or services are not initially competitive and have a slower maturation process. The initial rejection or little acceptance of the product will be reflected in a low level of sales.

Although "not all paths of disruption lead to success" ([10], p. 9), various authors argue that this type of innovation takes years to disrupt the market, but when they do, their growth is amazing. However, it is not without risk; for this reason, investors tend to be more conservative, since if the business does not work it would represent an economic loss for them and the company, associated with the high costs of research and development and the uncertainty of the results.

Based on the above, it is evident that uncertainty is one of the risks associated with innovation and that, in general, disruptive innovation is perceived as riskier than process innovation.

2.3.2 Differences in the duration of the startup life cycle

It had been argued that to analyze a company it is convenient to locate it in the stage of the business life cycle that corresponds to it, it was also previously mentioned that the life cycle shows business development through the evolution of its sales over time. In general, when a company begins -especially in startups- it goes through a **stage of development** of its products that it then submits to the market and begins **its introduction stage**. If the company exceeds its germinal stage, it will begin to develop its potential in the **growth stage**. Finally, the company will enter its **maturity stage** when sales growth rates slow (see **Figure 2**).

There is a close relationship between the life cycle of a company and the decisions of the type of innovation it wishes to undertake, and the life cycles of startups that develop disruptive innovations will be different from those that opt for process innovation; The product development processes will be different and consequently the investments to be made, which for example leads to the perception that disruptive innovation is riskier than process innovation and this fact alone will generate differences in the life cycle of companies that opt for one or another type of innovation.

It can also be seen that the disruptive startup causes the shift towards a completely new paradigm; however, this change is not immediate, since it involves the adaptation of consumers or the creation of a new market. For this reason, the introduction phase of a disruptive startup is usually longer than the introduction phase of a startup that focuses on process innovation, as shown in **Figure 33**.

The startup that innovates in processes presents a lower risk of market adaptation, since this type of innovation starts from an existing market that seeks to make the client company more efficient and competitive, but does not alter the final product or service. However, since the market is defined, the growth in product sales is limited by its demand, since the production rate must not exceed what the market needs. In this sense, the growth stage of the company that innovates processes is more limited than in the case of the startup with disruptive innovation, where the growth stage is more pronounced, since in this case innovation has the potential to create a new market. and thereby grow to a higher level. Once the growth stage is over, both startups reach their maturity stage, with the process innovation startup arriving first.

2.3.3 Investment level according to the type of innovation

Both in startups with disruptive innovation, as well as in those with process innovation, the investments made consider the research, development and implementation of the innovative idea, as well as the formation of the business, which defines its stage of development. Given that startups with disruptive innovation have a longer development and introduction stage, then investment levels will be higher for two reasons: first, because of the magnitude of the investment involved in developing a new product for the market and the longer investment period because while in process innovation the process to be optimized is known and therefore the research is limited, on the other hand, in disruptive innovation, research processes have to be

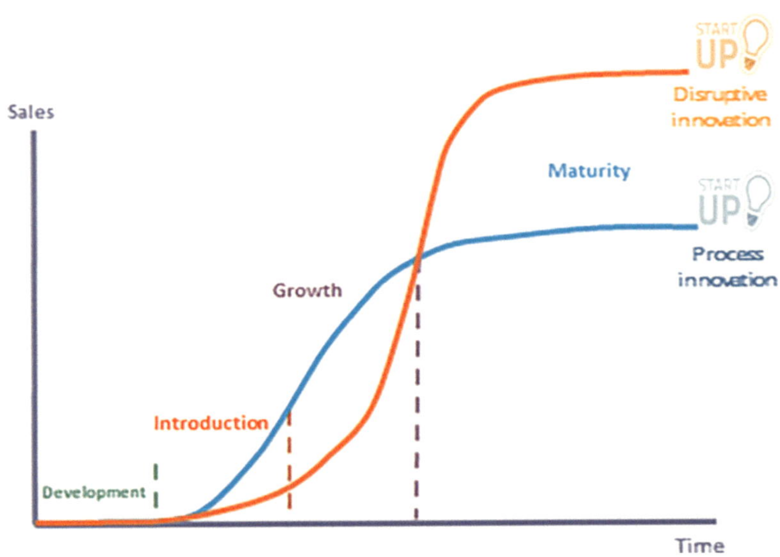

Figure 33.
Comparative cycles. Source: Prepared by the author.

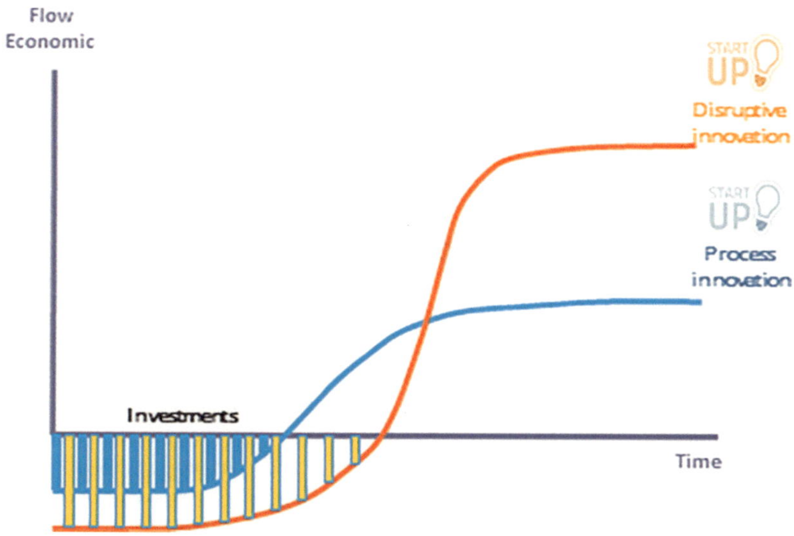

Figure 34.
Investment level. Source: Prepared by the author.

carried out with many hypotheses and test models, which mean a longer period of investment- This can be seen in the **Figure 34**.

2.3.4 Economic flows, profits and business value

In the previous Graph it can also be seen that the potential for generating economic flows by a startup that promotes a venture based on a disruptive innovation needs to be greater, since it must repay the larger and prolonged investments that the development of this type of investment entails. Products and for what should be done the analysis of the potential acceptance that it may have in the market. In process innovation, investments are lower and therefore market demands and economic flows are proportionately lower.

The profits of the business follow a similar evolution to that of the economic flows, possibly there are profits before having positive flows, but they will follow a similar trend. The previous considerations that have their origin in the business life cycle, which will correspond to each type of innovation to be developed, influence the process of valuing the company and the parameters to be used to calculate the value of shareholders' equity.

3. Discussion

The analysis of the life cycle of a business is the starting point for determining the projection of profits and cash flows, which are the basis for the valuation of companies. The construction of the life cycle of a startup makes it necessary to introduce a development stage prior to the introduction stage where sales begin, the reason is that these companies involve extensive periods of product development where investments must be made without still starting the commercial stage of the company.

The life cycle of a business represents the projection of sales of the company's products, in the development stage investments are concentrated to obtain a minimum viable product and then the expectation of initial sales of the product is represented describing the stage of introduction. Subsequently, the stage of expected sales growth is built and the projection ends with the configuration of the maturity stage, where the business is expected to grow at a slower rate until it has a growth rate close to zero.

This projection of sales multiplied by their respective prices allows the construction of business income, and these in turn the evolution of costs (semi-fixed and variable), of investments in fixed assets and working capital. With the information described, the projected Income Statements and the economic flows of the business can be prepared. Thus, the necessary information will be available to apply the methodologies to value the startup, by the net profit method or by the discounted cash flow method.

Properly constructing projections makes it possible to identify the necessary investment amounts, estimated investment times, and expected economic flows. These components make it possible to determine in advance the profitability of an investment and the value of a company. Although the projections made in the early stages are expected and possibly differ from the real ones, it allows modeling the behavior of the business that the investor will take as a basis to adjust his expectations of remuneration for his investment.

The development of the life cycle also allows the separation of two important phases of a business where two expectations of expected return -or discount rates- will be applied to value a business. On the one hand, the business incubation phase, which includes the development stage and the introduction stage. On the other hand, the consolidation phase, where the startup is expected to position itself in the market. Likewise, the cost of capital or expected return in the business incubation phase will be significantly higher, as it reflects the risk that, at this stage, the startup will not be able to position itself in the market. After this stage, the expected capital costs may coincide with the expected returns of a similar business in the market.

The life cycle is not the same for all businesses or startups, as it depends on their nature. For example, companies that invest in disruptive innovation products will have a longer development stage with longer and more intensive investment periods, but with the expectation that they will obtain significant growth once they are consolidated. This is different in startups that innovate specific industry processes, since their development stages are shorter, they have a known market, but also more limited since they are based on existing industries.

Finally, an analysis of the life cycle of a business that is evaluated from the development stage to its consolidation makes it possible to anticipate the levels of investment and to know what financing needs to look for in the different venture capital or investment funds. These investments can improve business expectations, but it also depends on the correct identification of this business life cycle, which allows an adequate risk analysis.

4. Conclusions

- By reviewing the literature, it can be identified that the life cycle of a business is made up mainly of three stages: introduction, growth and maturity. And this because generally the investment stages for the introduction of the products in the market have been of few periods.

DOI: http://dx.doi.org/10.5772/intechopen.110765

- In the study of the behavior of the startup, it can be understood that they have long periods until they reach the consolidation of the business. In the early stages they have losses and negative cash flows and it may be necessary to wait a long time until this situation is reversed. For this reason, this chapter incorporates one more stage in the business life cycle: **the development stage**, which precedes the introduction stage. During this period, investments are made until the sales that generate the first income begin.

- In **the development stage**, a series of investments are made until the company obtains a minimum viable product that is later incorporated into sales, thus beginning the business introduction stage.

- With the sales projection, it is possible to estimate the income, costs and expenses expected in the evaluation horizon of the startup, projecting the income statements and economic flows. Since the starting point is the sales projection, it is important to have an adequate market study.

- The projection of the Income Statements allows the startup to be valued through the Net Income Valuation Method or the PER (Price-to-Earnings Ratio) Method, which consists of updating the relevant Net Income that has a growth rate, at a cost of principal or discount rate.

- The relevant net profit of the business and its respective growth rate, which is used to obtain the value of the business, occurs when the company is in its consolidation phase after the development stage. When the business is considered consolidated, it is possible to value the company considering capital costs or expected returns. This is based on taking similar businesses as a reference or using PER (Price-to-Earnings Ratio) indices of referential businesses. Usually, Business Value is realized in a period after the development stage. If you want to know how much the value is at the initial stage or at the time the valuation is carried out, then you must update the value of the business previously obtained at a cost of capital corresponding to high-risk businesses.

- The Discounted Cash Flow Method uses the economic flows expected from the business, that is, the operating cash flow -income minus business expenses- also considering additional investments in fixed assets and working capital. With this method, the economic flows of the growth and maturity stage must be updated at a cost of capital corresponding to similar businesses. The previous cash flow and the development and introduction stage cash flows must then be updated to the expected return or cost of capital of high-risk businesses. The magnitude will depend on each case.

- In general, business life cycles based on disruptive innovation processes have life cycles with longer development and introduction stages, implying longer investment periods and where losses are expected to occur over a longer period of time.

- In general, in a startup that develops a product based on process innovation or frugal innovation, it tends to have relatively fewer investments because it supposes a substitution of a process that has an existing technology. This means that the new product has a better chance of becoming established in less time, taking into account that it already has a defined market but that it is also more limited.

Author details

Sergio Rafael Bravo Orellana
Universidad ESAN, Lima, Peru

*Address all correspondence to: sbravo@esan.edu.pe

References

[1] Fernandez P. Métodos de Valoración de Empresas. Documento de Investigación noviembre 2008. España: Universidad de Navarra; 2008. Available from: https://media.iese.edu/research/pdfs/DI-0771.pdf

[2] Tsorakidis N, Papadopoulus S, Zerres M, Zerres C. Break-Even Analysis. London Business School; 2010. Available from: https://library.ku.ac.ke/wp-content/downloads/2011/08/Bookboon/Economics/break-even-analysis.pdf

[3] Schmookler J. Invention and Economic Growth. Cambridge, MA: Harvard University Press; 1966. DOI: 10.4159/harvard.9780674432833

[4] Sherman G. Technology Transfer Innovation and International Competitiveness. Houston, United States of America: John Wiley & Sons, Ergodebooks; 1981. ISBN 10: 0471084689; ISBN 13: 9780471084686

[5] Malerba F, Orsenigo F. Patrones de innovación schumpeterianos. Cambridge Journal of Economics. 1995;**19**(1):47-65. DOI: 10.1093/oxfordjournals.cje.a035308

[6] OCDE. Disruptive Technologies and Regional Innovation Policy. Broadening Innovation Policy: New Insights for Cities and Regions. 2018. Available from: https://www.oecd.org/cfe/regionaldevelopment/KoutroumpisLafond(2018)Disruptive%20technologies%20and%20regional%20innovation%20policy_FI.pdf

[7] Bonilla E, Diaz B, Kleeberg F, Noriega M. Mejora continua de los procesos: Herramientas y técnicas. Lima: Universidad de Lima, Fondo Editorial; 2020. p. 2020. Available from: https://repositorio.ulima.edu.pe/bitstream/handle/20.500.12724/10832/Bonilla_Diaz_kleeberg_Noriega_Mejora_continua.pdf?sequence=1&isAllowed=y

[8] Danneels E. Disruptive technology reconsidered: A critique and research agenda. Journal of Product Innovation Management. 2004;**21**:246-258. DOI: 10.1111/j.0737-6782.2004.00076.x

[9] Bass R. Disrupting ourselves the problem of learning in higher education. 2018. Available from: https://4cast.uiowa.edu/sites/4cast.uiowa.edu/files/DisruptingOurselves_Bass.pdf

[10] Christensen M, Raynor M, Mcdonald R. What Is Disruptive Innovation? Twenty Years after the Introduction of the Theory, we Revisit What it Does—And doesn't—Explain. Harvard Business Review. 2015. Available from: https://hbr.org/2015/12/what-is-disruptive-innovation

[11] Govindarajan V, Kopalle P. The usefulness of measuring disruptiveness of innovations ex post in making ex ante predictions. Product Innovation Management. 2005;**2005**:13

[12] Hang C, Yu D, Cheng K. An exploratory study on understanding the technological dimension in disruptive innovation. In: The 5th International Symposium on Management of Technology (ISMOT'07). 2011. Available from: https://www.researchgate.net/profile/Kah-Hin-Chai/publication/242122624_An_Exploratory_Study_on_Understanding_the_Technological_Dimension_in_Disruptive_Innovation/links/564139d808aeacfd8936480c/An-Exploratory-Study-on-Understanding-the-Technological-Dimension-in-Disruptive-Innovation.pdf